Morgan!
Many Blessings

INSPIRATION FOR
AUTISM

A Pathway to Hope and Resources

for a beautiful journey!

Debra Dilley Rosen

Deb

WESTBOW
PRESS®
A DIVISION OF THOMAS NELSON
& ZONDERVAN

WestBow Press books may be ordered through booksellers or by contacting:

WestBow Press
A Division of Thomas Nelson & Zondervan
1663 Liberty Drive
Bloomington, IN 47403
www.westbowpress.com
1 (866) 928-1240

ISBN: 978-1-5127-4951-9 (sc)
ISBN: 978-1-5127-4952-6 (hc)
ISBN: 978-1-5127-4950-2 (e)

Library of Congress Control Number: 2016911302

Print information available on the last page.

WestBow Press rev. date: 07/28/2016

Reviews for *Inspiration for Autism*

I sat down to read *Inspiration for Autism* on a beautiful Friday afternoon, not expecting to complete the entire book in one sitting. It captivated my heart and took me on quite a journey. My spirit soared, I laughed with Mrs. Rosen at times and cried in others. Not only did she unleash her emotions for other parents to see, but her spiritual journey was challenged as well. Never has a book about a child with Autism covered so many areas. The story is beautiful, but I was specifically drawn to her expert knowledge incorporating a hands on model to access medical, behavioral, and educational services needed for a child with Autism. I would love to include this book as a required reading for my graduate students earning a Special Education Credential ... it's that good!

—Shari Harris, PhD,
autism specialist, educator

Debbie offers hope for parents managing Autism in their family by sharing her own personal journey with her Autistic child and providing practical information. Her transparency of revealing deep personal pains and family challenges are overcome by yet a deeper faith in Jesus Christ that brings understanding, healing and optimism for life.

—Andrew Bosco, associate pastor,
First Baptist Church in Orlando, Florida

Her book is lovely, heartfelt, sweet, honest and extremely helpful. And Anthony ... he is so blessed to have her for his mom. Unbelievable!

—Sandra Keays, MFT

I believe this book could help so many people who have or know someone with Autism. I have worked with Special Needs Children for over seventeen years and was educated in many ways to help understand the needs of Autistic kids. I would strongly suggest this book for the insight of a mothers journey, new ways of coping with the situations one will encounter, and help others to know these kids are just like any other child who wants to feel accepted and loved the way God made them.

—Debbie Osterman, special education
Instructional Aide

Mrs. Rosen takes the reader on a personal and honest journey of one mother as she navigates the diagnosis of Autism, its treatment, the educational system, and the complexities of family life. Her story is one of faith, family, hope, advocacy, and persistence.

—Heidi Glesne, M.S., BCBA
(board certified behavior analyst)

I was completely drawn into Debbie's remarkably honest memoir. She explains how she has coped and what she has learned of her son's Autism diagnosis. She offers great advice on resources and how to stay sane through it all. Thank you, Debbie, for giving me hope. I wish this book was given to me when Autism first became a part of our lives.

—Pilar A. Gallagher, mother of two daughters
(one with autism)

To my cherished daughter,
Allison.

I love you with all of my heart.

Contents

Acknowledgments

I extend my most sincere and heartfelt thanks to my daughter, Allison. Without your smile, conversations, grace, and love, I would be adrift. You bring the entirety to our family. You are truly the sweetest gift from heaven, and I love you with all of my heart.

I thank my son, Anthony, for his courage and willingness to overcome his innermost struggles. You have been nothing short of an inspiration to me. You bring such joy to my life, and I love you with all of my heart.

I thank Rob, my husband, who asked to share in my expedition on earth. Your encouragement, love of life, and fortitude help me more than you will ever know. Your willingness to keep fighting the good fight is honorable and treasured. My heart is yours.

Without exception, I thank every behavioral therapist who helped us on our own individual journeys. You know who you are, and this book would not have been possible without each and every one of you. Nor would I. Your patience, wisdom, and heart carried me through many difficult days. You transform lives, not just autistic ones.

I want to especially thank each and every one of my dear friends who took the time to add their own flavor and wisdom to this particular project. Linda Durbin, Heidi Glesne, Shari Harris, Debbie Osterman, Pilar Gallagher, Andrew Bosco, and Sandra Keays, you have helped me to see different perspectives that were hidden from my viewpoint. I am humbled by your willingness to show me how community works together for His kingdom.

I thank my editor, Holly Lorincz, for such foresight and intellect on my beloved manuscript. You have helped me to share my heart and my experiences with the very people in need of hope and inspiration. You change lives.

I thank my mom, dad, sister, and other family members for helping me have confidence in myself and in my dreams. Without my solid foundation, I would not have been able to build my indefinite future. Your investment in my life will be forever cherished.

I want to thank my dear girlfriends. Without all of you, I wouldn't be all of me. I am blessed to be able to live life with each and every one of you. Thank you.

I thank my heavenly Father. You are my everything. Always.

Introduction

My daughter is a *typical* developing teenager with those *typical* teenage behaviors. (If you have one, you understand those italics.) My son, on the other hand, is not your typical teenager. He is a boy with special needs. He was diagnosed at around age three with autism. Put yourself in my place. Do you know how to raise an autistic child? Neither did I.

I have been blessed because my heavenly Father has given me two children, and I love them for exactly who they are. The struggles we have faced are not unique to our little family, yet autism still seems like a hidden disease with a stigma for the child, the parents, and the brothers and sisters. I believe it is important today with the climbing rates of autism in our society that we understand the shoes each family member walks in. From the heart and the head of a single mom who left behind a career to raise an autistic child, you will see the private tears, the fears, and the work needed to change different maladaptive behaviors, how to help siblings understand their challenging roles, and how to help the school provide an education for your special child.

My career has always focused around education. I began teaching high school at the early age of twenty-three. I simultaneously worked during the summers at a local university, teaching at the New Teachers Institute for hopeful young educators. I loved teaching high school; however, with the completion of my master's degree and school administration credential, I soon was hired as an assistant principal at a junior high school not far from my home. I learned invaluable skills working with staff, students, and parents during my career in administration. I also enjoyed the leadership role as part of the vision of our staff and teachers. It was an exciting career, and every day brought new challenges and new lessons.

As I was climbing that career ladder on the way to becoming the next principal of my own school, I was given the blessing of motherhood. Raising two children and putting my ladder climbing on hold was one of the best decisions of my life. Then it became apparent that I wouldn't be climbing my own career ladder anymore, as I'd be traveling down a new road instead and picking up a new ladder. My son's developmental disability was diagnosed, and autism entered into our family.

With that diagnosis came a wealth of information I hadn't imagined existed. I became a parental expert on the subject by experiencing it firsthand and then by applying the techniques I'd been taught in addressing it. The onset of this journey was frightening because I knew so little. Thankfully, God has guided me through each step. Now I pray for each parent to have strength and faith, facing the same fear that paralyzed my first steps. This book is a result of that prayer, and it also reveals my desire to hold out a helping hand to you as you begin your journey.

In the hopes of sharing my challenges, difficulties, gifts, and rewards, I focus on my story as a mom walking through the diagnosis of her only son. My yearning is that I can leave you with a hope, an inspiration, and even some encouragement. There have been so many gifts and blessings we have received *because of* and not *in spite of* this diagnosis!

The second part of my book is a resource section with educational questions and concerns that may arise with special needs children. It is written from my perspective as a mother, teacher, assistant principal, and parental advocate for my son. It speaks of inclusion in the general education population, IEPs, and "not fitting in" with the other kids in the class and on the playgrounds.

My prayer is that you find the *hope* and not the despair in everyday living with your family. I hope that you find the *joy* and not the fear as you travel down unchartered roads. I hope that you *enjoy* your life as it has been given to you and not long for another. I do not believe in coincidences. I believe you're reading this book right now, and it is part of God's perfect plan. Enjoy your journey as I have learned to enjoy mine!

Blessings,
Deb

Part 1

OUR STORY

Chapter 1

OUT OF THE SILENCE

It was a cold, rainy February day when we walked into our pediatrician's office. I was concerned that my two-year-old boy didn't speak or even grumble, mumble, or make any sound that slightly resembled a word.

My pediatrician examined Anthony quickly like he had always done before and said, "He's fine. He's two. His older sister speaks for him. He doesn't need to speak for himself. Don't worry, Mom, Anthony is a typical, active, little guy!"

He tried to get Anthony to mimic and imitate him and was mildly successful, so he concluded, "No problems, no concerns." Yet I was insistent we see a speech therapist. My boy was close to three years old and didn't have any intelligible speech. He didn't come when I would call, and I was concerned he might be deaf as well as possibly speech-delayed. I expressed my concerns and was adamant on the issue. The doctor wrote the referral for a speech pathologist who practiced at the hospital where Anthony was born. Thank God for that referral. We were soon to meet one of the most influential people in our lives, Ms. Renee.

I remember walking into Pomona Valley Medical Center and signing my silent boy up for speech therapy. My daughter, Allison, and I navigated Anthony through the frightening world of clinical speech therapy without his dad present. Allison and I would enter, and Anthony, of course, would storm in as usual. I had in hand my staple backpack with toys, picture books, small handheld computer games, cheese fish, and juice cups ready for any moment Anthony might need a change of activity.

Ms. Renee was one of the nicest people we had ever met. She greeted us in the lobby and took us back into her therapy room. I was scared to death. I was intimidated that Ms. Renee and other professionals knew about speech disorders and other disabilities that I knew absolutely nothing about. I felt completely out of control and out of the safe, cushy world that I had built for myself. I was also afraid of needing services to help my boy with what I believed was such an easy skill—talking. I soon learned that communicating and talking isn't that easy to acquire when you have a disability in that area. What is easy for one is not easy for all. In addition, without talking, the world is a very limiting space.

I vividly remember how she taught my quiet boy how to talk. It was a painstaking and a grueling amount of work and effort. She used blocks—one green and one red. We sat on the floor, and being the brilliantly observant therapist that she was, she realized he was insanely interested in blocks. She held one in each hand and refused to give them to him until he made a grunting sound to ask for them. She explained to me that language is a two-way form of communication. One speaks, and then there is a reaction from the other. That reaction could be speaking or an action of some sort. She realized Anthony had not made that connection. He had no idea that if you made a sound, then something would happen for you. His brain did not understand the basic fundamental connection of cause and effect. His brain could not comprehend that when he made a noise, that sound caused an action to take place. If she could get him to grunt to get the block of his choice, then he could make the connection that sound equals action. Once he would understand that his sound equaled an action, the next step would be forming and molding that sound into syllables. Once he understood syllables, she would have to mold and shape those syllables into words, and voilà, he would be speaking. Sounds like a simple task, right? The process is grueling just to describe. Imagine a repetitive learning system … daily. It was quite the challenge. Maybe for some children it is an easy task, but not for my silent son.

Grunting didn't come easily. I remember screaming fits for the entire fifty-minute speech session because Anthony didn't get the item Ms. Renee was using as a bribe. She refused to give him anything until he would stop crying and make a normal sound. Sessions went by. He wasn't the only one crying at the end of those grueling days. I cried a lot too. I brought toys and books for Allison and tried to shield my daughter as often as I could. It was hard. I remember working full-time during these days and making speech therapy appointments on Saturday mornings so I would be able to get him there. While his dad was off to the gym, I would pack both kids in the car after working forty hours myself, and off to speech we would go. This was both physically taxing and emotionally draining for me.

Then one day it came—a grunt of normal sound. The green block was given to him immediately. Every time he would grunt, another block was given. He would soon connect in his brain that his grunt sound equaled getting the toys he wanted. The first lightbulb went on. Ms. Renee slowly shaped his grunting into syllables and *gah* became *green*, and the green block was given as his reward. Syllables became words. It went slowly, very slowly. Session after session and many endless hours of practicing at home became our new normal. I soon realized that although the fifty-minute speech session was invaluable in teaching speaking skills to Anthony, I would have to emulate those speech sessions endlessly at home. In fact, we practiced at Grandma's house, at the store, in the car, at school, on walks, in the backyard, in his bedroom, while watching television, and while eating at the dinner table. It was exhausting. I was the pseudo speech therapist in charge of my silent son's vocabulary development. Please do not misunderstand me. Therapy sessions are extremely vital. In fact, they're crucial, but for many autistic children, that is only the beginning of the work involved. It is a twenty-four-hour-a-day, seven-days-a-week, thirty-some-days-a-month effort to continue to make progress with many of these kids. Some children pick up skills and generalize them more quickly than others. Each child is very unique. Like snowflakes, none are alike. My child took many months to speak, and as a teenager, he continues to have many deficits in this area.

I also vividly remember being introduced to the PEC system. PEC stands for picture exchange communication. If Anthony could hand me a picture of a preselected item, then he would get that item. Because autistic children may be extremely visually intelligent, Pictures could help them learn to communicate. So I blended this PEC system with Ms. Renee's hard-nosed grunting system and didn't give Anthony anything he wanted until he handed me a picture of it or grunted for it.

I kept pictures of household items, toys, and food labels in a box for him, and I sat him down to show him if he wanted the apple juice, he'd have to hand me the label I'd pasted on the index card. If I was given the index card, then he would get the apple juice. I would tape Cheetos and Cheerios to index cards and have a box of index cards available for him to choose from. I would lock the pantry. Yes, I installed a lock on the pantry door because I wanted to be in charge of everything he might possibly want. He eventually learned that he had to hand me a card for everything from the TV remote to the Cheez-Its if he wanted something.

Tantrums multiplied. You can imagine that if you had free reign of the home one day and then couldn't get or have anything unless you worked for it, how frustrating that might be. Speaking was his challenge, and now he would have to stop, think, process, and create an action of some sort before getting his most desired items, food, and toys. It was extremely difficult for him. It might feel the same if I had to approach my biggest challenges in life and couldn't eat or relax until I did. It was like a power struggle between the food and the grunts, and guess who was in the middle of it? It was stressful to be the wall between him and his toys. In fact, it was difficult on the entire family. I often went to bed at night crying because of the emotional strength it took to get through the day. I lay awake, questioning my decisions in regards to my son. I often worried about being too tough on him. Every time I asked the professionals, I always got the same response. I was doing all I could possibly do to help my son speak. I buckled down, thanked my son's therapists, and said my prayers.

Eventually, his brain did make the connection that communication had to happen if he wanted to get something he desired. *I have to go to this delusional lady I call Mom and hand her this card or grunt to get that delicious cookie I could have just grabbed yesterday freely without talking to anybody. This sucks,* he must have reasoned. Thus, the tantrums.

The tantrums were long, hard, and loud. Eventually, the card system worked, and he would attempt to hand me a picture for everything he wanted and needed. Then we had to step it up and have him hand me the card and make some attempt at the word. He had to do both simultaneously. More tantrums and more frustration accompanied the more difficult task. We would have to stretch him yet again. He then had to turn the grunt into the first syllable of the actual word. When he mastered those skills, he had to say the first part of the word. It sounded like *Che* for "Cheeto," *jew* for "juice," *mi* for "milk," etc. He had to get very close to the first syllable to get what he wanted.

Imagine the tantrums again! This took months. This was extremely frustrating for my son. Finally, we graduated to the entire word. "Cheeto" gave him the Cheeto. "Juice" gave him the juice. "Milk" gave him the milk. This took many more months, and the tantrums continued. But finally, he was using words to get what he needed. Slowly but surely, he was talking. It was a long process with tons of protests, but he was using his words! He was using our words! He was communicating.

At two and a quarter years, when he began speech therapy, he had been completely silent. Now at three years and ten months, he had ten words. I was so excited for those ten words, even if he was almost four.

He now speaks. He makes his grammatical errors, and his conversational skills are delayed; however, he can ask for anything he desires. He uses his verbal skills much like any typical kid does, though he is still delayed by a couple of years, according to his speech therapist after his assessment. But I need to keep in mind that he really didn't even speak for the first four years of life. I am hopeful that as he continues to grow and learn, the gap will be less and less. Pictures, grunting, syllables, and delaying his desires until he worked for them helped my silent son to be the chatterbox he is today.

- Patient people like Ms. Renee have helped my son tap into places in his brain where he did not want to go.
- The Lord, who was holding my hand, helped me to be strong when I wanted to give up so many times.
- The chocolate-brown, tear-filled eyes of my boy begging me to help him gave me the determination to persevere.
- The words that came slowly gave me the hope that there were so many more hidden inside him somewhere.
- Perseverance, hope, determination, and faith are such wonderful gifts.

Learning the Signs of Autism

The following is taken directly from "Autism Speaks," a nonprofit organization determined to help spread the awareness of autism by providing a wealth of knowledge and resources for parents and others alike.

The following "red flags" may indicate your child is at risk for an autism spectrum disorder. If your child exhibits any of the following, please don't delay in asking your pediatrician or family doctor for an evaluation:

- No big smiles or other warm, joyful expressions by 6 months or thereafter.
- No back-and-forth sharing of sounds, smiles, or other facial expressions by 9 months.
- No babbling by 12 months.
- No back-and-forth gestures such as pointing, showing, reaching, or waving by 12 months.
- No words by 16 months.
- No meaningful, two-word phrases (not including initiating or repeating) by 24 months.
- Any loss of speech, babbling or social skills at any age.

Learn the Signs of Autism. (n.d.). Retrieved March 17, 2015, from https://www.autismspeaks.org/what-autism/learn-signs

Chapter 1 Review

This is your takeaway:

- A parental instinct is very strong. Trust yours. If you feel something isn't right, it probably isn't. Seek help.
- Encourage language from your child as early as possible.
- Praise your child for every attempt at speaking and communicating.
- Buy a drill if necessary.
- *Never give up!*

> *But you, man of God, flee from all this, and pursue righteousness, godliness, faith, love, endurance and gentleness. Fight the good fight of the faith. Take hold of the eternal life to which you were called when you made your good confession in the presence of many witnesses.*

> *—1 Timothy 6:11–12*

Chapter 2

ONE EYE OPENED ...
ONE EYE CLOSED

When people ask me if I recognized the signs and symptoms of autism in my son when he was a toddler, I tend to say that I had one eye opened and one eye closed in terms of my son's development. I would look at him and think, *Well, he is putting puzzles together ... and he likes to investigate things. He must be fine. If there were something wrong with him, he wouldn't be able to put puzzles together.*

I understood that he didn't speak verbally and that his nonverbal gestures were nonexistent as well, but I would explain that away. *Well, his father is kind of quiet and shy. He must take after him. He is very independent, and he even gets his own milk at age two! If he really had an issue, then he wouldn't be able to process pulling up a chair to the kitchen island and helping himself, now would he? He must be okay.*

I should have known that *typical* developing children would ask their mommies to get their juices or their "baba." They would say, "Mama," or perhaps cry, whine, or gesture to attain their desire. Not my son. Not my very quiet son. My son was not doing any of those things. I would often justify this, thinking, *Anthony is such a smart, independent thinker that he is pulling up a chair and getting his juice all by himself. Or look at him pulling me by my finger and showing me what he wants. That's great development. That is good processing. That is completely typical with an edge of intelligence, in fact. He's fine. He is perfectly normal!*

The problem was that he did this all alone. He did everything independently of his mother or his father. He did it silently. That was my first clue. I missed it. Or did I? One eye opened and one eye closed.

It is so difficult for parents to know what typical development looks like and what may be signs of a bigger issue brewing underneath. Compound that with the fact that sometimes parents take their children to pediatricians and receive conflicting opinions about early childhood development. We as parents are taking our children to professionals, banking on the fact they know everything about diagnosing disorders. Doctors have been formally trained and spend years educating themselves in childhood development. These professionals must know what they are speaking about and what they are diagnosing and what they are not. Parents may put their faith in what their children's doctors are stating because they don't feel they have any other option. They may feel they don't have the same formal education, so they rely on their pediatrician's words. However, I do believe it is necessary to state that doctors *practice* medicine. Perhaps they are not experts in every diagnosis of every childhood disorder. That is what occurred in my son's case. My son's pediatrician didn't see the early warning signs of autism. It could have been attributed to the fact that autism wasn't as prevalent as it is today. It may have been the fact that autism is a wide-spectrum disorder, and because Anthony seemed extremely normal in some areas, the doctor overlooked the weaker areas of development. Whatever the case, I took his word with a big sigh of relief because after all he was the professional. My son didn't have autism. The doctor confirmed my hope. My fears were put aside for a short while. Parents, formally educated or not, may cling to the idea that if their children are growing in some areas, then they must be developmentally on the mark. They may say to themselves, *Perhaps my child is a bit slower in some areas than others, but nevertheless, he's okay. Everybody grows at a different pace, so I'm not going to be concerned. He is the second child and has everything done for him, so he is going to be a bit slower at learning things. He's a boy, and boys develop slower than girls. But he will catch up.*

I was no different. I didn't understand the term "scattered skills," meaning kids do not develop one skill after the next in an escalating fashion. They develop skills at different rates at different times, not in a typical forward-moving fashion. Scattered skills are very common in these children. They may be extremely bright and creative in one area and extremely poor in some others. His life was filled with scattered skills. For example, although he had an extremely well-developed skill in pulling up a chair and helping himself at age fourteen months, he didn't speak out loud or ask for help with this task. He could put puzzles together at an alarming rate but he couldn't point to the bird in the sky when I asked. He had a phenomenal memory of navigational directions and recall regarding where places were located. (He would cry if we passed the off ramp to Disneyland.) However, he lacked the ability to gesture, to shake his head yes or no, and to come when he was called. As a parent, I would cling on to the extremely bright areas and hope the poor skills would catch up miraculously. One eye opened and one eye closed.

The poor skills didn't miraculously catch up. He was silent. He didn't begin to gesture to things. He didn't look at me in the eyes or even in my direction when I called his name. He just didn't seem interested in many things for very long. He lined up his cars and trucks in an odd fashion. He seemed different. But he did his puzzles with ease, and he watched and laughed appropriately at *Baby Einstein* videos and *Barney* cartoons. He seemed to hum a perfect pitch to music and dance like Fred Astaire. He even seemed to play appropriately with some toys (*some* being the operative word here). *He is doing well*, I would reason. I would hope over and over again.

Our trips to the park would bring new discoveries for all of us. I would often take my son and my typically developing daughter to the park to enjoy the day with each other and others who might be there. Although he always wanted to be around the other children, he really never played with any of them. I understood the concept of parallel play, the idea that children play in close proximity *to* one another but not necessarily *with* one another. I also understood it to be for kids under the age of about two and a half. However, my son was fast approaching four, and he only engaged in parallel play. He would play right next to the others and seem to enjoy being around them, though I never witnessed any interaction. Most young children pass the sand bucket or at least claim it with authority. Anthony did neither. He was content playing alone, looking at the sand run through his fingers as though he was *investigating* it. Other children didn't seem to bother him; however, they didn't seem to interest him either. One eye opened and one eye closed.

Daily errands that every busy mother needs to accomplish would soon bring new concerns. The outings to the grocery stores, gas stations, department stores, and other shops would eventually shed some light on my strong-willed child's temperament. My daughter, Allison, who is twenty-one months older than my son, would accompany us everywhere we went. If we were in a hurry, which every Mom knows is almost every day, Allison would go with the flow. She adapted easily. She would hurry up when Mom would hurry. If for some reason we wouldn't be able to enjoy that yummy cherry slushy, she would, for the most part, understand. Some whining, protesting, or complaining might occur as with any youngster who was deprived of that yummy, tasty treat, but no matter what her age, the tantrum was usually under somewhat control. It was short-lived. It was over in a typical fashion. It really was never intense or obnoxious.

My son didn't seem to have the same idea about shopping. If we would be rushing around, he would not "go with the flow." The yelling and screaming would begin. If we would go to that same yummy slushy store and accidentally left our change at home, his tantrum would rock the world. Distraction didn't seem to work. When his mind was set on something, it was that item or hold on to your seat. Other oddities included rigidity on the shopping aisles. If we would go down a particular aisle in the grocery store, we would have to go down that same aisle in the same fashion, or Anthony would crumble. No deviation was allowed. I had no idea why this happy, silent boy would be totally fine one minute and a blubbering mess the next ... and quickly. I later learned that having a predictable routine was key in the lives of some of these autistic children. He was absolutely great on the shopping trips that were routine and in place, but when we deviated, he was a disaster. It seemed to me, an educated parent, that he was having an off day. We all have those. That's what I would tell myself, and I reasoned away those shopping days. I would often say, *It's a bad day, or maybe he's hungry. He's a boy, and he is two, so he's doing exactly what two-year-old boys do—tantrums. It's perfectly normal.*

You know, those things we tell ourselves when we have one eye opened ... and one eye closed. The stories are countless. They will unravel in the future chapters as they unraveled in our lives, illustrating further the premise that I was prone to keep one eye opened and one eye closed, holding dear to Anthony's strengths and dismissing his weaknesses. Every loving parent sees their children through the lens of perfection and beauty. I was absolutely no different.

What I know today is that my son was made perfect, all of him, even the silent parts. He just needed tools, strategies, programs, determination, and hope to help him learn to navigate this world. Each night I would tuck my children in with a sweet kiss and a warm "I love you." With her big, beautiful, ocean eyes, my daughter would look up at me when she was young and say, "I love you too, Mommy." With his big, beautiful, chocolate-brown eyes, my son would look up at me in silence. I would shed a tear, sometimes more, hoping one day he would say, "I love you too, Mommy." But he would lay silent, staring up at me for years.

Those silent good nights eventually turned into typical evenings of kisses and words from both of my children. After learning various approaches to teaching Anthony how to speak, we finally got to "I love you, Mommy" and so much more. The main purpose of my book is to provide you with those same skills, to help you with advancing your sons and/or daughters in their various needs. Speaking was one of the numerous challenges my son had to face. After numerous trips to assorted professionals, Anthony received the diagnosis of autism. That diagnosis explained the silent nights and other irregular behaviors we faced. That diagnosis, as hard as it was to receive, opened up a whole new world of information, therapies, and resources that would eventually help diminish his negative behaviors and increase his positive ones. With resources and information came knowledge. With knowledge came the hard work. With the hard work came "I love you, Mommy." We continue to have those meltdowns. Some days those meltdowns are short-lived, and other days they are more intense and last longer. Some days I prime my boy about what the day is going to look like, and other days I stretch his frustration tolerance and say, "Let's see what the day brings." Some days are more rigid and organized, and emotions run smoothly. And some days are rigid and organized, and emotions rage. It seems somewhat typical to me as I write this. And finally, there is not a day that goes by now during which I do not hear, "I love you, Mom," from both of my perfectly made children. Sometimes my boy tells me more than once a day. And now both of my eyes are opened, and I am grateful for what I see and for what I hear. I am thankful for what I have been given. I am blessed with the two gifts I have been chosen to raise this side of heaven. I am loved, and so are my children. We always have been.

Chapter 2 Review

This is your takeaway:

- Keep both eyes opened.
- Learn the developmental milestones.
- Always get a second opinion from other professionals if you feel the need to.
- Don't explain away the strong-willed behaviors.
- *Never give up!*

Consider it pure joy, my brothers and sisters, whenever you face trials of many kinds, because you know that the testing of your faith produces perseverance. Let perseverance finish its work so that you may be mature and complete, not lacking anything.

—James 1:2–4

Chapter 3

A HARD LOOK IN THE MIRROR

There I would be washing dishes, answering the phone, finishing that load of laundry that never seems to end, and instructing my children all at the same time. Wow, did I take pride in my multitasking. Then there would be Allison in her three-and-a-half-year glory and Anthony with his one and a half years, multitasking themselves. After all, they watched Mom do ten things at once, so why shouldn't they? So there he would play, moving from toy to toy, not spending much time or interest on any one item for an extended length of time. He would also line up small toys for no apparent reason over and over again repeatedly. He never made any car sound while playing with his numerous cars, which I always found a bit bizarre, considering every little boy his age did make those sounds. Books would lie all over the floor, sometimes torn into pieces, while educational videos that were created with the "development of children" in mind would play in the background. We were a busy family.

"Anthony?"

"Anthony?"

"Anthony?"

I would call as I was finishing that last dish or word on the phone.

"Anthony?"

"Hey, T-bone?" I would often call him that, but it never elicited an answer. I wouldn't even get a visual reference or a look in my direction.

Actually, I had many names for my son—T, T-bone, T-bony bolonese, just to name a few. Looking back at it, no wonder I never got eye contact, he probably didn't even know what his name was. All kidding aside, eye contact—or a lack of eye contact—was apparent from an early age. Lack of eye contact is a significant early indicator of pervasive disorders that I was ignorant to at the time. That will be addressed in more detail in a later chapter.

It didn't matter if I was multitasking in the kitchen with the phone in my ear and my hands in the sink, calling out for Anthony, or visiting the park with other mothers, the kids running amuck in the sand. I would unknowingly be teaching Anthony *not* to listen to me. I remember another episode on a warm, sunny morning at the park around the corner from our house. We'd often walk with our tricycles, sand toys, and snacks, a seven-minute walk to a quaint park with a playground, a grassy area, and seating benches. I'd tell Anthony over and over again, "Don't ride too far ahead of me. Stay close," only to be ignored as he rapidly accelerated down the sidewalks. I would continue to chase after him, yelling out, "Slow down. Stay with us, Anthony!" Again, I was teaching my son he could continue to ignore me because all I would do is yell out and there would be no consequences. Looking back, I should have taken the tricycle away and turned around to go back home if he couldn't listen. But as many moms do, I wanted to avoid the behavior that would accompany that decision and not ruin the day for my daughter, who had been looking forward to the outing. So I continued to yell out, and he continued to ignore me.

Of course, it didn't end there. We'd be at the park, and moms would be chatting together while their kids would be playing happily. If one mother needed to tell her child something, she'd simply call out his or her name, and the kid would usually jaunt on over.

Not me.

Not us.

I'd call out for Anthony numerous times while he was lost in another world in the sand. He'd be so focused and so intent on his sand toys and his sand mess, he'd never even think about looking in my direction, let alone come over. So again, I'd call out numerous times while other moms looked over at me, wondering why my kid didn't look in my direction, let alone mutter, "Yes, coming, Mom," or even say, "Not yet."

Why did I do that? you might be asking yourself.

To avoid tantrums.

To fit in with others.

To not make a scene.

To not crumble the day for my daughter.

Because it was too much work.

Whatever the reason was, it was a hard look in the mirror. Humbling.

Nevertheless, there I would stand, calling out his name numerous times with only silence returned. Little did I realize I was actually teaching him not to listen to me or to my words. You see, when you call out a child's name once and then you don't get a response (either a physical one with him coming over or a verbal one of him saying, "What?" or even a visual referencing look at the very least), then you as a parent may be tempted to call out his name again. If it takes three times to evoke a response, then that child learned he doesn't have to listen to his mom until the third time she calls him. Nevertheless, he is learning not to listen.

As a loving mom who was very busy keeping a house and holding down a job, I would often do this unknowingly. I would teach Anthony indirectly that he did not have to pay attention to me until I got tired of saying, "Anthony?"

"Anthony?"

"Anthony?"

Then I would raise my voice or walk over to him. It has been termed "learned behavior." A learned behavior is a behavior (him not attending to my response in this scenario) that he learned from me. Hence, the term "learned behavior." Later after much training on behavior interventions, I realized that I could contribute to some of his challenging behaviors with my parenting style. *Me?* It was a hard look in the mirror. After all, I loved my children very much and strived to make the right decisions for them daily. How could I, an educator for God's sake, be teaching my child *not* to listen to me?

Oh, I see clearly now. I was supposed to say, "Anthony?" one time and one time only. If I did not get a response, I was to go over to him, kneel down at his level, and stop him gently from his activity and say, "Anthony, I am talking to you." And then proceed with my interaction with him.

That would require me to stop and think every time I was addressing my child and be able to follow through. I would need to be able to stop what I was doing and physically walk over to him to evoke a response for my conversation with him. This simple behavioral tactic actually seems to work on everybody. If completed consistently, it tends to elicit a first response from both typical and special needs children. It even works on adults. Imagine having your husband say, "What, honey?" the first time you called out his name even when he is watching his favorite television program. Miraculous. Well, not really. Just consistent behavior strategies.

Typical children, for obvious reasons, pick up on this a bit more quickly. I practiced my new skill of saying "Allison?" only one time, and if I didn't get a physical or verbal response on her part, I would go over to her and say, "Excuse me. I'm talking to you, sweetheart. Let's try that again." I'd walk away and go back to the same spot where I originally called her from and say, "Allison?" She would turn her head and say, "What, Mommy?" Then I would pour on the praise, "Great job listening when I called you," and proceed with my direction or conversation. Allison, being typical, picked up on my new parenting tactic fairly quickly. I was proud of how she would politely and respectfully answer me when I spoke to her. What an amazing listener she became.

I would *target* listening everywhere I went with the children. I would pour out the praise each time she answered after one call. Allison became a great listener. I would be more thoughtful in my words before I spoke them. Anthony, on the other hand, didn't pick up on this skill so easily. As I will share, our behavior training didn't begin until after about age three and a half. Prior to that age, I would continue to unknowingly teach my children not to listen to me when I spoke to them. There we would be, multitasking in our daily lives, not spending too much time on any one thing. I would be multitasking myself and unknowingly teaching my children to do likewise. I was teaching them learned behavior all along the way. You see, I would take pride in teaching them the *good* learned behavior. The *good learned behaviors* are those things like picking up their toys, sharing, sportsmanship, and taking turns. I was proud that they were learning what I taught them. Little did I realize that they were learning the things I didn't formally teach along the way. Both of my children watched me closely and learned the good, the bad, and the ugly. They were learning both sides of that equation. They were learning the things I would formally teach them and the things they would randomly pick up.

Some parents choose to use the "counting to three" model for discipline. If the parent gets to three before the child complies, then the child is in trouble. That model also teaches kids in a very subtle way that "they don't have to listen the first two times the parent is talking to them." So parents will go around the grocery stores, parks, and playgrounds and count to three, sometimes counting all day long. Seems like a lot of wasted time and a lot of counting. Wouldn't it be nice to speak once and have the child respond? That would be a very nice display of shared communication between child and parent.

As I learned my new skills, Anthony learned his. Funny how that works, huh? As I grew and adapted, Anthony grew and adapted. I have concluded that I had to change my response to Anthony if I expected Anthony to change how he responded to me. I had to start with me. I had to change my parenting style. I had to stop multitasking and start having higher expectations of good behavior from my children. I had to begin to model good behavior myself. I had to slow down if I expected Anthony to slow down. It wasn't easy, but nothing good is ever easy. There is an old saying that goes something like, "If you want to change the world, you must start with yourself." I thought that meant everybody but me. I was perfect the way I was. It turned out to be a very humbling experience.

I remember reading somewhere that in marriage counseling, couples who struggle the most are the ones who go into counseling with a list of reasons why they are right and their spouses are wrong. They are the ones who work very hard at proving their point to the other's demise. It is a bit saddening to think they are supposed to be on the same team, looking for a win-win instead of a "I win, you lose" solution. It's much like that with parenting. It's not about how I am right because I am the parent and you are the child. It's more like this: "Let me see what I can possibly be doing to cause my child to do what he or she is doing. Let me take that hard look in the mirror and grow so my child will grow." I prayed for guidance and wisdom a lot in those early months. The Lord answered with gentle reminders of my own character flaws. As I asked Him to chisel me, somehow miraculously, Anthony and Ally were chiseled as well. It's not that hard to look in the mirror when you know He is right there to help.

On most days when I say, "Anthony," my beautiful boy stops what he is doing and comes over to me, smiles, and says, "What, Mom?" Coincidentally, on most days I have learned to say what I mean and mean what I say. I really do not believe in coincidences. Learning to take a hard look in the mirror has been a really good thing not only for my children but for me as well. I am glad I didn't have to do that alone.

I offer blessings to each of you so that you experience much self-growth on own your journeys.

Chapter 3 Review

This is your takeaway:

- Say what you mean and mean what you say.
- Remember, they learn the good and the bad of what they observe.
- Your child is more important than your ego. Parent everywhere you go.
- If they don't listen to you, they won't listen to anybody else.
- *Never give up!*

> *My son, if you accept my words, and store up my commands within you, turning your ear to wisdom and applying your heart to understanding~ indeed, if you call out for insight and cry aloud for understanding, and if you look for it as for silver and search for it as for hidden treasure, then you will understand the fear of the Lord and find the knowledge of God. For the Lord gives wisdom; from His mouth come knowledge and understanding.*

> *—Proverbs 2:1–6*

> *Trust in the Lord with all your heart and lean not on your own understanding; in all your ways submit to Him, and He will make your paths straight.*

> *—Proverbs 3:5–6*

Chapter 4

DENIAL IS DANGEROUS

To accept your child as disabled and having a label placed on him really goes to the core of a parent's soul. With a label, reality seems to set in. This becomes a new journey and a new future for the entire family. What now? It can be pretty scary. Ignorance is bliss, I once read; however, denial is dangerous. It is dangerous for this disorder in particular because early intervention is key when dealing with the development of the brain. The earlier a child is diagnosed and treatment begins, the better the chance of a *typical life* for that child. According to the numerous volumes of research done on early intervention treatments and their findings, children being treated at early ages seem to sustain the benefits far greater than those who begin treatment later in life. Just as children can learn a second language as babies in a bilingual home, they will be more fluent as they speak that language than they would if they learned it in a high school Spanish class.

Bringing the disorder into the light and coming to grips with the fact that my child needed help—more help than I alone could provide—was a life-changing event for me. Oh, how our lives changed. Being an educator brought a bit of confidence to my parenting skills. To admit to myself that I wasn't enough was challenging to both my ego and my soul. *How could I not be enough for my own child? How could someone who knows and understands kids not know how to deal with her own? How could someone else know my child better than me?* These are some of the questions I would ruminate on over and over as I faced the fact that Anthony might have a disability.

When Anthony was originally diagnosed as having a developmental disability, he was about three years old. Regional Center, an institution that provides services and/or funding of services for people with developmental disabilities, such as autism and cerebral palsy, was one of the resources I tapped into. Most counties have a Regional Center, but parents need to be assertive in finding them. I also learned a lot from very helpful parents I had spoken to. I learned that I should place my requests for services in writing to every institution I would be dealing with. Placing your requests in writing begins a *timeline* for the institution to respond in a *timely manner*, which is a sound idea. If parents do not put their requests for assessments or services in writing, an institution may not be legally obligated to respond. Another perspective is to trust that people and entities set up to help those in need will be working in the best faith effort of your child, which is naïve. Though this may be true for some institutions, sadly, this more often may not be the case. Funding is slim, and those whose needs are intense and whose parents' voices are *legally loud* are the ones who seem to secure the services.

"Put requests in writing," has been my hallmark, and people seem to take me seriously. I have sent requests via certified mail with a return receipt. It is one more way to prove that your requests have been sent and received. An organized tracking system from day one of this journey has been vital to navigating this *goose chase*. I bought a simple notebook and began the ever-grueling documentation process. I documented whom I spoke with, what institution, the time, the date, and the key points of the conversation. There were so many conversations that this process helped me to get all of the information out of my head and onto paper, organized in one book.

- Put every request in writing.
- Mail every correspondence certified, including a return receipt for the document received.
- Save every e-mail sent, and keep a hard copy for your files.
- Get second and third opinions from all professionals in dealing with diagnosis, treatments, and therapies.
- Research services and interventions available in your county and your state.
- Get your own assessments from your preferred practitioners, and use them in all meetings.
- Keep a log of all of the important people you spoke with along with the times, dates, and key points.

Regional Center was my first stop. I requested they evaluate my son's condition. The first evaluation occurred in my home. Two psychologists arrived and explained to me that since Anthony was so young (age three), they would sit, play, and observe him. I allowed the interaction while I remained in the room. They took notes and evaluated Anthony by watching his play style. They stayed in my home for a total of about two hours. I remember being very anxious to know what they had observed. I asked them for their opinion concerning his development, but they were not allowed to offer any verbal diagnosis at the time, though they did say (and these words are as loud today as they were many years ago), "Your son is severely developmentally disabled." *So much for not giving me any professional advice*, I thought. Wow, what a blow to hear in my home with my daughter by my side and my silent boy lining up his blocks in an odd fashion. His dad was busy at work, and I was processing this alone. They told me they would be in touch, and then they left. I was devastated.

What do I do? Who will help? What's the future going to be like?

What does this mean for my boy? What does this mean for my family? What does this mean? The questions raced through my mind as the tears streamed down my face.

That day began the *great divide*. I jumped into my son's diagnosis, determined to find help, while my husband firmly held tight to the belief he would be fine and that he would grow out of it. What happens when you and you partner suffer the great divide? Read chapter 10 ... twice. Support each other, and get help to do it. It is a difficult road to travel alone.

Nevertheless, the Regional Center offered Anthony an early-start class. This early-start class met two times a week for one-hour sessions. Every member had a disability of some sort, and the teacher and one aide had to deal with a multitude of issues and concerns simultaneously while trying to teach skills. It was quite the task. We soon figured out this placement was not going to be sufficient enough to meet our son's needs. It was, however, my first eye-opening experience to a variety of disabilities. A world I never thought I would personally have to navigate.

After speaking with the regional center, I do not remember being offered any more services for Anthony or our family. Regional Centers have a variety of services for different disabilities; however, as I soon realized, it is the parent's job to research those services and know what questions to ask. Those who do not seek do not receive.

Anthony finished the year in his special day class (SDC) and found some structure in his unstructured world. Looking back, I remember how hard it was to for me to see my vivacious boy sitting in a class that seemed so below his academic level on some skills and so above his level on others. He seemed to move quickly through subjects he liked, such as numbers, colors, and letters. Concrete, visual pictures and ideas seemed to work best for him as well. Sitting was just plain difficult. We would later realize he had attention deficit hyperactivity disorder (ADHD) along with a few other issues that will later be discussed. Hence, the challenging journey of sitting and learning simultaneously began.

Anthony finished the year with some progress, and I believe that I finished the year with some as well. I learned I had a long road ahead of me. I learned that this was going to try my patience and my strength. I found out this was not going to happen overnight, and it was going to be much more of a process than a quick fix. I learned that I, too, had ADHD. (I can laugh about that now.) I learned I could be quite emotional and sometimes irrational at times. I learned that I was human.

I also believed that two hours a week of instruction were insufficient to develop the social, communication, and academic skills that were sorely absent in my son. I knew he would need much more intervention than the Regional Center special day class could offer. Hence, I began a mass search for services to help my son.

As time has progressed and so have the skills, Anthony is currently in a regular general education classroom with typical peers. He began with a one-on-one aide who shadowed him through his day, helping him where he needed it. We faded that aide support over time, which is called a transition plan. He is meeting most academic standards, and he enjoys going to school. His strongest subject has consistently been math. Reading comprehension has proven to be very difficult for him, and we have recently incorporated a specialized reading intervention program to help bridge the gap. It has been a constant challenge to choose whether his academics or his social skills should take precedence in his education. Many parents may opt for academics. However, for us, I chose a class of typical developing peers as a priority. I have implemented supports for Anthony to *help* his academic skills, including an aide, a modified curriculum, intervention programs both in a resource specialist class and on computer software programs, and tutoring by both peers and adults. However, in the end I wanted to model typical peer interaction for Anthony so that he learned from others, felt consistent high expectations placed on him, and learned to live in the world in which I lived. A general education class with appropriate support seemed to be the best placement for my son.

Labels, diagnosis, and prognosis are such intimidating words. My philosophy is not to worry about the terms but instead to find the help your child might need and to not cease looking. Regional Centers and SDC classes were only the beginning, as you will see. As you, too, will learn.

I kept myself organized with a notebook of conversations, and I documented everything I said and heard. I put my requests in writing, asked questions of everybody, sent correspondence by certified mail, and began a mission to locate services and professionals to help my son. It is a full-time job in and of itself, but it can get done. Determination, patience, hard work, and a lot of prayers and faith have been my stabilizers. And at the end of each year, every teacher has told me he's not the same kid as he was in the beginning of the year. Progress and growth are such great gifts. I am so grateful for my many gifts.

Chapter 4 Review

This is your takeaway:

- Ignorance is bliss, but denial is dangerous.
- Put every request in writing.
- Early intervention is crucial.
- *Never give up!*

Now to Him who is able to do immeasurably more than all we ask or imagine, according to his power that is at work within us.

—Ephesians 3:20

C h a p t e r 5

SENSORY OVERLOAD

Recently, a famous clothes maker decided to take the tags off of the inside of the T-shirts. The company then began printing the size denominations in ink and replacing those nagging tags that always seem to irritate the back of our necks. Many designers followed this simple idea. *Poof*—that irritable tag was gone! Amen. That seemed to solve one of our nagging issues at home, cutting off every tag of every jacket, sweatshirt, T-shirt, and pajama top in my little boy's closet and drawers. But then there was his "I don't want to wear jeans and jackets" (even if it's raining and the dead of winter) because "I don't like the heaviness on my body" syndrome. This was closely followed by the "I don't want to walk on the sand at the beach" because "I don't like the texture on my toes" issue. Not to forget the movie theater that was unbearable complements of the "it's too loud" fallout. However, Barney, the big purple dinosaur, couldn't be turned up loud enough because of the "I can't hear him" problem. There have been far too many issues, problems, and syndromes to recall in regards to Anthony's hypersensitivity to touch and sound.

I really think I noticed Anthony might have had sensory issues when we were having a barbeque with friends in our backyard. Kids were running around, yelling and laughing and genuinely having a good time. There he was about two and a half years old, walking along a two-foot-high retaining wall on the patio—one of those toddler activities that parents tend to cringe at yet allow at the same time. Then every parent's nightmare occurred. He fell off of the retaining wall and onto his back, and his head directly hit on the concrete floor. Everybody stopped in that terrifying moment as I ran over to pick him up as quickly as I could.

Not a peep.

Not a cry.

Not a scream.

Not a tear.

In fact, he looked at me with a puzzled look as if to say, "What's wrong with you, Mom?" He had a huge goose egg on the back of his head, yet he didn't even seem to notice he had fallen in the first place. It was like he didn't even feel pain. I was as shocked as everybody else at the barbeque. It was bizarre. Remember that earlier concept of the "one eye opened, one eye closed" thing? I was thinking, *Oh, wow, tough boy. Great! Oh no, what was that crazy event?*

The idea that my son could fall on his head onto concrete and not feel that pain was terrifying to me. I knew something was not right with that scene. How could he not feel pain the way I did? It was like his pain barometer was off. It seemed like he had no measurement for feelings. His measurement for pain, emotions, light, sound, and other senses was very different, and so was his output of reactions.

Some physicians and therapists refer to this phenomenon as sensory integration dysfunction. The idea is that the body receives input from our senses, such as eyes, ears, physical touch, etc. If the sensory input is too much or even too little, then symptoms such as inattention, fidgety movements, and impulsivity can be observed in some children. Some doctors believe that for some people, the amount of input coming into their bodies and their senses is too fast or perhaps too slow. A trained professional might be able to spot this by the patient's particular behaviors. For Anthony, inattention, overly excessive fidgety movements, and impulsivity were very apparent from the beginning. In addition to those behaviors, other sensory integration (SI) symptoms were observed in Anthony as well.

They included the following:

- Holding his hands over his ears because of loud noises. These behaviors were often seen in movie theaters and concerts.
- Avoiding bright lights and putting his head down, especially in the sunlight.
- Avoiding eye contact initially, even people he was familiar with.
- Avoiding many foods (a whole chapter by itself).
- Consistently hanging on to and bumping into people. He seemed to be unaware of his own body and the proximity of it to other people and objects.
- Poor endurance for any sustained period of time.
- Constantly jumping, running, and moving his body. He seemed to have the inability to stop physically moving … ever.
- The fascination with feeling people's skin. He seemed to like the texture and the softness of skin, which seemed to be very apparent early on.
- Difficulty paying attention.
- Difficulty standing still and being able to *be*.
- Being overly anxious.
- Having no sense of control over his emotions (overreacting and underreacting).
- Having an unusually high tolerance for pain.

Perhaps a parent may look at this list and think that some of these are symptoms of a typical two-year-old! Perhaps some of these symptoms can be portrayed as a developing, busy, inquisitive toddler boy. But the intensity of them seemed to be the deciding factor for Anthony. His behaviors were intense. They included all of the above to the tenth degree. One therapist definitely diagnosed him with sensory integration disorder. His neurologist labeled him with ADHD (attention deficit hyperactivity disorder). I personally didn't care about the name of the diagnosis or the label of the disorder. I was far more interested in the treatment and care. I was more concerned with lessening the intensity of normal everyday sound and sights for my son. As God closes one door, He always opens a window. This window was accurately named occupational therapy, otherwise known as OT.

Ms. Lynda was our first of a few different occupational therapists. She was extremely helpful for this part of Anthony's developmental journey. Occupational therapists are trained in helping patients engage in activities that help people with events in their daily lives. Occupational therapists help with self-care skills, education, and social interaction skills. Ms. Lynda taught us how to have him use his big gross motor muscles in activities, to help balance out his internal body senses. Trampolines, bike riding, and swimming were all tactics we used to help regulate his senses. They actually seemed to help him regulate the sensory overload that his body was experiencing. "Work him hard and wear him out" was the motto. What did that look like in reality?

- He would carry big bags of groceries in the house.
- He would push full boxes of toys in the playroom.
- He would carry objects up and down the stairs.
- He would jump on the trampoline for ten to fifteen minutes daily.
- He would ride bikes, scooters, and anything else with wheels around the block daily.

- He would go running.
- We put our two-year-old to work and try to have fun in the meantime.

She had us on an extreme exercise regime that seems sort of silly as I read and write this. Every active toddler naturally burns energy in a normal and healthy manner. Anthony was a very active toddler. In fact, I could not ever get him to sit still. To deliberately make him carry heavy items or jump continuously to burn even more energy was exhausting for both of us. It was fun and games when he got to do what he wanted to do, but when I deliver the message, it's not fun anymore. It's work. A few challenges met us along the SI occupational exercise path, but nevertheless, the heavy gross motor routine continued with the other therapies simultaneously.

In terms of helping Anthony adjust to loud noises, we had to begin where Anthony was first comfortable. We had to allow him to learn how to tolerate louder noises, but we had to do this at a slow pace. For example, if we wanted him to be able to listen to the television in the house at a normal level for most people, then we had to discover what his normal level was. If he was able to tolerate the volume on the TV at a ten on Monday, then we would turn it up to an eleven on Tuesday. We would keep the level at an eleven until he was comfortable and he learned to tolerate the increased level. We then would progress to a level twelve until he was able to tolerate it. We would continue this regiment until a normal volume range could be tolerated in the house. It was a very tedious process, and it taught our family to be very patient. Over a period of time, Anthony was able to tolerate the same level of noises in most places, including movie theaters and other loud events, as others would. Concerts continue to be challenging, and every once in a while, I will catch him covering his ears. However, the progress has been great, and Anthony has learned to listen to sounds in our world and not just his.

We practiced the same slow-paced regiment in terms of learning how to tolerate more light—one lamp at a time. Then there were two lamps and so on. The key was slowly pushing forward each day. I had to constantly remind myself I wanted Anthony to live in our world and that I didn't want to live in his. If I did not push the limits on lights, we would be living in the dark today. The same goes with the volume. Noise doesn't stop in this world because one person has an issue with it. If I wanted Anthony to live a typical life, I had to constantly encourage him to adapt to our world every day and in every situation. It was a slow process that took a lot of patience, determination, and faith.

He also struggled with certain textures, such as sand. He would stop at the boardwalk of a beach and sit and scream. He couldn't deal with the sand between his toes or the texture of little rocks and seashells under his feet. I would find that the more I enabled him, the more rigid he would get. If I would hold him across the sand, the more he wouldn't push himself to go across it by himself. Inevitably, the more I would join his world, the more he would stay in it. So I had to combat that by slowly engaging him in our territory and hearing his scream all of the way through it. If it was the beach, I would begin by holding him for part of the experience. Then he needed to walk it. Walk it like everyone else. I would actually let him scream on the sand and slowly walk away and direct him to follow. The therapists shared with me my son would follow because he didn't want to stay by himself. This was a very difficult task for me. I had to trust he would come when I started walking away. I did this with help, of course. The therapists would stay behind in a place he couldn't see so that he was safe from my end as well as from behind him. I would give the direction to him to follow across the sand and start walking away with my daughter in tow. He would sit and scream, and I would keep walking. Eventually, as I stayed strong and didn't look back, he would start to walk across the sand and fight his own anxiety to catch up. The therapists were not far behind, so

I knew he was completely safe. I also attempted stunts like this with my mom and friends so that I always felt confident he would be okay. Therapists or not, there was always a family member or a friend willing to help me work on the goal I was trying to achieve. Find them. Ask them. It does take a community to raise a child, especially on the spectrum. He learned that I meant what I said and that his screaming fits didn't work anymore. He had to follow and fight through his fears and dislikes. Like it or not, it was the only way he would adapt to any type of normalcy. And adapt he did. Slowly, he departed from his world and joined ours.

In my devotional book, I read that it is good to leave your children some battles. Parenting children is often like walking a tightrope. It is a balancing act of rushing to save them from hurting themselves and making mistakes and then allowing them to learn from their failures. I saved Anthony from a lot of his own mistakes early in his lifetime. I did not want to see him cry or struggle. It was difficult for me. I fought a lot of his battles for him by carrying him across the sand, fixing the meals he wanted for dinner, cutting off those nagging tags on his clothing. I didn't allow him to learn to fight his own struggles in life. God allows trials in our lifetime. He wants to grow us, and He allows small and large battles to cross our paths. He allows us to learn from our difficulties and challenges. He wants us to learn to see life through His perspective and not our own. I am learning to allow Anthony the same respect. He is learning to fight his own battles instead of having his mommy fighting them all for him. He is special and needs special help from time to time. But he also needs to learn how to fight his own anxieties and frustrations. He, too, is learning to lean on the Lord and not on himself or me.

When Anthony was first diagnosed with autism, it occurred at the Regional Center by the psychologist on staff. There is no medical test that can diagnose autism. Because it is a complex disorder, the diagnosis usually encompasses parental questionnaires, psychological assessments, speech, and occupational reports, and the DSM-5. The DSM-5 is the *Diagnostic and Statistical Manual of Mental Disorders* used by professionals to classify people who may be on the spectrum. Some categories observed in the DSM-5 include social interaction, rigidity, and communication. The tests given can be a bit subjective based on the evaluator and the parental observations, so it's extremely difficult to say for certainty how severe Anthony really was when he was first diagnosed.

He was low in many areas. "Your son has autism."

Crushing, loud, thundering words.

Then, of course, came the need for a *guarantee* of what life would look like for him in his future—the same *guarantee* all parents want for their children only intensified. There are no guarantees. No doctor or professional could tell me how far in life my little boy would make it. There is such a broad range of outcomes for individuals on the spectrum. Some will speak, and others will not. Some will develop slowly with much intervention, and others will begin learning on their own. Every child is different.

What seems to remain constant in the research available is that early detection and early intervention is key to unlocking this disorder. One of the reasons I share such intimate details of our lives is to hopefully have you reflect upon your own. It's also to offer you the techniques I have seen work over time with my son's overall progress. I pray you see them work in your child's life as well.

Thankfully, now we go to the movies monthly and sometimes weekly. We enjoy sitting and eating popcorn like everybody else. We watch those loud, action-packed movies with a few bouts of ear-covering, but that's easily redirected with encouragement and praise. I don't always remember to cut off those annoying tags anymore. Nor do I have the need. The lights are not a problem like they used to be. He even puts the sunshade down in the car if the sun is too bright. The beach is his favorite pastime, the sand and all. His attention span is a continuous work in progress and perhaps will always be. But that is part of his life ... and part of mine too. He's a boy, and he is enjoying life. And we don't need any more guarantees because we have learned there aren't any in this life ... except for one—the Lord.

Chapter 5 Review

This is your takeaway:

- Avoiding lights, sounds, and textures is a bright red flag.
- Find an occupational therapist who understands sensory issues.
- Begin stretching their tolerance for light, sounds, and textures from where they begin and move forward from there—slowly but steadily.
- Be patient and remain determined.
- *Never give up!*

> *As for God, his way is perfect: The Lord's word is flawless; he shields all who take refuge in him. For who is God besides the Lord? And who is the Rock except our God? It is God who arms me with strength and keeps my way secure.*
>
> *—Psalm 18:30–32*

Chapter 6

AND THEN THERE WAS FOOD

Food—that delicious, flavorful, scrumptious commodity we place in our mouth and savor every day. It seems simple enough to place food in front of children and expect them to gobble it up as we adults do, right? Wrong. Typical developing toddlers go through that selective, picky stage. You remember that stage, where they would avoid anything green on the plate at all cost. It's the stage where most parents bribe their children to eat their veggies first before they can get any dessert, the stage where parents may sneak healthy snacks on the plate and in the lunch bags. In fact, the stage is so well known that some food manufacturers include sources of vitamins and servings of vegetables in their food products.

In some autistic spectrum children, picky isn't even the right word. Fussy, particular, and hypercritical don't even hold a candle to how choosy my autistic son was with food. Anthony had a diet consisting of about five items in total. In other words, he would only eat a variety of five different food items all day and every day. Green wasn't an option. He wouldn't even consider healthy snacks. It was a diet of five items, and none of them were vegetables. *Selective* and *discriminating* are more the words I would choose to use in describing Anthony's eating habits.

When he was between one and two years old, he did enjoy a variety of toddler food—fruits, veggies, cheese goldfish, proteins, milk, and Cheerios. This seemed to be a typical diet of a young toddler. However, as the months passed, he would start to develop an adverse taste to pretty much everything except carbohydrates. I believe eating processed foods triggered this. I remember allowing him to eat French fries from various places, and that is precisely where the selectiveness began.

He narrowed his diet down to a select few items, such as waffles, granola bars, pasta, chicken, and French fries. He absolutely refused to eat anything else. Not wanting him to starve, I fed into this limiting diet of his preferred dietary items only. Later when taking a hard look in the mirror at myself, I realized that was a poor choice of mine.

I vaguely remember as a child having a plate of food put in front of me, and being expected to eat it. Imagine that—one meal for the entire family, and if we didn't finish it, it suddenly appeared at the breakfast table the next morning. As children, we were told to eat what was in front of us and show our gratitude for a hard-cooked meal, even one that included veggies. Oh, and that old saying "You won't get dessert until all of those peas are gone" was often sung as I was growing up. Why that concept of mealtime didn't get passed on to my children, I'm not quite sure. I think I was too busy fighting Anthony's battles for him at that time. But separate meals and favorite dishes became common as my children were small and demanding. "How do you undo that?" you may ask. Well, it wasn't easy. In fact, it took about nine months of a broken-down food program and therapists in my home to undo the damage of giving into separate meals and preferred items only. This is how I remember it.

Like I had alluded to previously, Anthony had deviated to a few preferred items only. Those items had to be brought with me when we left the house because he wouldn't eat anything else. Imagine taking your family to a nice restaurant to enjoy the evening and then breaking out the baggie from the pantry to satisfy a demanding child who refused to eat restaurant food. I *concreted* Anthony's strong will. I allowed his will to be stronger than mine. I fought his battles, and he was the one actually losing.

When our behavior therapy began, I shared with his therapists this major food dilemma. *Poof*, a food program was utilized. Imagine needing a food program from behavior therapists to undo what I helped to create in the first place. We had to use his very favorite food as a reinforcer to encourage him to eat other foods. At that particular time, it was those delicious soggy French fries from our local In-N-Out Burger fast-food restaurant. I had to go and purchase one order each day of therapy. These French fries in essence were the bribe to help me teach Anthony to tolerate different foods. Much like the therapy with sound and light toleration, we had to start right where Anthony was. At that time if he had something green on his plate, he would gag, throw his plate, scream, hit people, and throw his food up. We had to begin there. We had to teach him to tolerate having food on his plate first. Then he needed to learn how to touch it without those behaviors and then smell it without those behaviors and then put it into his mouth without those behaviors until he would begin to eat it and not gag. It was an exhausting journey.

In the therapy program, Anthony would get French fries if he would simply allow me to place a vegetable on his plate. I wanted to be able to give him veggies, fruits, and a variety of meats and carbohydrates, but one thing at a time here. If he could tolerate the green bean on his plate without whining, crying, or throwing a tantrum, then he could have all of the French fries. This sounds simple enough, but the key phrase is "without those behaviors." However, looking at that monstrous green bean would send the dish flying across the room. No French fries would be rewarded, and a major temper tantrum would occur. He cried, screamed, and threw things for hours. We tried the toleration of that green bean on the plate daily until he could do it without any tantrum. Many days later he accomplished it. He allowed that green bean to sit on his plate without a word or complaint. The French fries came as a reinforcer, and he learned to tolerate food on his plate without a tantrum. A reinforcer could be a toy, a treat, or a star on a calendar. It is whatever your child will work for in learning a new skill. Step one completed! He learned to tolerate food other than *his* food on his plate. Great, now we had to step up the plan to "touch the green bean," or he would get no French fries. The process of throwing the plate and tantrums began all over again. We had to stay on that step until he could touch it without crying. Bingo, mission accomplished. That took about another month.

Step 3: Pick up the green bean. Tantrums began.

Step 4: Smell the green bean and put it down. Tantrums began.

Step 5: Lick the green bean and put it down. Tantrums began.

Step 6: Put the green bean in your mouth and spit it out. Tantrums began.

Step 7: Chew the green bean and spit it out. Tantrums began.

Step 8: Chew the green bean and swallow. Tantrums began.

As you can see, it was quite the process.

A lot of French fries were purchased. A lot of tantrums occurred. It took a lot of patience, determination, and time. However, nine months later, he finally ate that disgusting green bean.

Finished? Not quite. That was only a green bean. There is a lot more food in the world besides green beans. We had to do that process daily with every food item I wanted him to eat. Food time became fight time. It was miserable for my daughter and for me. I always did this without my husband in the house, as he could not tolerate the tantrums and throwing and spitting of unpreferred items. It was a long and lonely process. We progressed, and the fighting started to cease. The therapist taught me it would always get worse before it would get better. It's always darkest right before the dawn. Behaviorists term this difficult period as an "extinction burst." Once he realized that we weren't going to back down, he ate the food. He fought to the ends of the earth (to an extinction burst), but my will had to be stronger than his. My food had to stay even when it was thrown across the room. My food had to return even if he gagged. I had to outlast him. The behaviorists were correct. It was a battle of the wills. I won the battles. He won the war in the long run though. That's what all of this was for—so my son could have a healthy variety of food without the whining, complaining, and crying. Nine months of difficulty for a lifetime of variety.

I eventually had to move to the next stage of our food program. It was stage two. That consisted of allowing him not to eat what was on his plate and respecting his wishes. However, he'd see that same meal the next mealtime. If the shrimp scampi didn't get consumed for dinner, guess what breakfast was? That's right, shrimp scampi. Sometimes that shrimp scampi was heated up four different times before he'd eat it. That didn't taste very delicious, I'm guessing. He began to learn, "Wow, it is better the first time around." Phase two worked. He began to eat whatever I put in front of him the first time. This is the stage my parents started at for me. This is the stage that didn't get passed from one generation to the next. This was another hard look in the mirror for me.

The behaviorists who came into my house weekly worked on his maladaptive behaviors. The food program was only one. They assessed him and put goals into place that would help him diminish the negative behaviors and increase newly acquired, more socially appropriate ones. They were also very costly and expensive to obtain. In later chapters I will address how I secured their services and how I found which ones would best work for our family. The therapists helped to pinpoint the problem areas, but truly, I tell you, I had to do the daily work with my son to see the change of behaviors. Having therapists come into my house helped tremendously, but if I didn't keep up the therapy after they left, it would have been futile.

As you glance into our lives and delve into my stories, you may think, *Where did all of these therapists come from anyway?* After much research on early intervention for autism, I constructed a list of therapies other parents had found helpful for their children on the spectrum. You will find this list in the later chapters of this book. I specifically hired and researched thoroughly the applied behavior analysis therapists. I even interviewed other parents who had utilized them, and I observed them interact with my son too. After feeling confident with them, I requested my son's school district and our local Regional Center pay for in-home services. I provided private clinical assessments supporting the need for such intense services, and I put my requests in writing. Today many health insurance carriers are mandated to provide behavioral services to children with autism. In addition, some parents privately fund these services for their kids. Because of the extreme financial burden it can become, I would suggest checking your health insurance carriers, local Regional Centers, and school districts for what services are available that you may be able to obtain.

The food program was a very difficult stage in Anthony's journey. It entailed a lot of work on my part to undo what I had created. Looking back, I had allowed and actually encouraged my son's finicky appetite. I enabled him to be picky and choose his meals. I even brought his favorite foods along to restaurants to avoid the tantrums and the scenes. It was a war on many fronts. A war I almost did not win. It was a war that would eventually wind up dividing our home. My boy could have won, but he would have lost. Better to fight the good fight than to sweep issues under the rug ... or *green beans* for that matter.

Now waffles, pasta, granola bars, chicken, and French fries are only a few items we eat in my house today. Salad, shrimp, steak, broccoli, and carrots are also some items we consume weekly. We continue to struggle with some soups and stews, but hey, if there is something green on that plate, I'm excited. Oh, and by the way, I don't carry food around anymore. I have left the baggies at home. If Anthony doesn't like what is on the menu, he skips that meal. Today, he is a growing boy who is always hungry. It's funny how he never skips a meal.

Chapter 6 Review

This is your takeaway:

- Don't make different meals for different family members ...*ever.*
- Eat your veggies before your dessert ... *always.*
- Be cautious of processed foods.
- *Never give up!*

   Let us not become weary in doing good, for at the proper time we will reap a harvest if we do not give up.

   —*Galatians 6:9*

Chapter 7

WALK YOUR TALK

He will stop doing what he is doing, when you mean what you say! "I do mean what I say!" *He's yanking your chain because he can. He's getting away with things because you let him; because he knows you allow it.*

"You mean he will straighten up and behave when I do?"

Exactly. When you change your behavior, he will change his.

What a revelation that was. This sounds vividly close to the conversations I had with my son's therapists over the course of his behavior therapy. They would share with me the old adage, "Say what you mean and mean what you say every time you speak to him." Although I believed wholeheartedly I said what I meant, my behavior wasn't always consistent. Those holes were the inconsistencies my son would feed on.

Say what you mean and mean what you say is a simple enough concept, right? This constant advice from the therapists brought hope that my son could learn boundaries. He could learn right from wrong. He could cognitively understand what was being spoken to him, and he could be closer to a typical learning toddler. We might be able to go out in public and have him listen to us and behave. We could possibly have a more normal life. This was a blessing that brought hope, but the action and results that followed brought conviction.

Behavior therapy began in our home when Anthony was three years and eight months old. I had completed much research on ABA (or applied behavior analysis) and the benefits many families saw in this type of therapy. I had learned about this particular kind of therapy by doing some Internet research, talking with other parents, reading numerous books, interviewing many agencies that used this technique, and speaking with various doctors and professionals trained in dealing with special needs children. ABA is a specific therapy approach that deals with breaking down skills for children in the smallest, simplest form and highly reinforcing the positive behaviors that follow. In other words, it was a team of trained therapists who worked on specific skills Anthony was weak in. They assessed him to see where he was developmentally in many different areas and then proceeded to slowly teach him from that point and progress forward.

They taught him through one-on-one direct instruction, bringing his skills up to typical developing levels. They would concentrate on reinforcing those skills when he was correct and ignoring or "extinguishing," as they said, his incorrect responses. The therapists defined this approach to teaching an "errorless" approach. They wanted to ensure that the patient's brain wanted to work for positive outcomes versus gaining attention through negative consequences. This therapy is research-based, and it tends to increase positive outcomes and minimize negative behaviors.

This therapy is intense. It became our new normal. We had a team of five different therapists who had specific goals they would work on. They entered our home right after school, and many times stayed right through dinner. Our family time was invaded. Our private time vanished. Our family dynamics and environment forever changed in order to save our son's life.

Each therapist brought their own style and personality to our home, though the basic therapeutic practice was the same and consistent across therapists. They would consistently reinforce the good behavior and extinguish or ignore Anthony's bad behaviors. Anthony learned if he wanted positive reinforcement, he had better follow the directions that were given. In fact, if he wanted any reinforcement, he would need to do as he was directed. Some children act out even for negative attention. Any attention is reinforcing for them. It was a hard concept for me to learn that some kids would do anything if it would grant them a reaction, good or bad, from their parents. This errorless approach would grant attention only when a positive response was given, thus encouraging Anthony to seek out positive attention versus negative attention.

Positive reinforcement would include such things as verbal praise, stickers, food treats, hugs and kisses, time on the computer, TV time, games, etc. Anthony's preferred items, such as Play-Doh, music, paint, and others, would be rationed when he would meet his goal and work hard for the session or for the day. If he wanted that Play-Doh, he knew he'd have to work hard to earn it. At first I thought this was bribing my child into submission, paying him off for behaviors he should be already doing. Those behaviors would include such simple tasks as sitting still, listening, being quiet, paying attention, and giving eye contact. I would often ask myself, *How will my son ever learn to behave because it's the right thing to do if he is rewarded for what he should be doing already? How will he ever do the right thing because it's the right thing to do?*

As you are reading this, you may be asking those same questions. However, I learned that Anthony didn't really care about doing the right thing just because it was the right thing. Some people are born as pleasers and receive pleasure, joy, and happiness from doing the right thing and pleasing others in the meantime. Anthony was not born a pleaser type. We had to teach him right from wrong and show him that by doing the right thing, good things can happen, including things like watching his favorite television program or computer time. We also had to teach him that doing things that are not right would bring consequences and boundaries.

The hope was that after he learned and utilized enough skills, he would begin to transfer his emotions and reactions to more of an intrinsic motivation. This was a hard concept for me to grasp, motivating my kid through items. This is not old-school thinking. This was hard for me to implement, as I had come from such a strict disciplined family. But I tried it, and I saw results. Anthony began following directions. He began to comply with instructions. Slowly but surely, he began to understand what was being asked of him. The results were the proof, and my skepticism began to slowly fade. I tend to look at this approach to teaching skills differently today. I have asked myself the questions, *How many people get jobs because it makes them active members of society? How many people get jobs because they get paychecks every month?"*

Maybe we don't work for Nutter Butters or Goldfish, but I would bet most of us work for wages.

An example of ABA in action is clearly demonstrated in the directive "Come here." These therapists were the ones to teach me the correct way to get my son to come the first time I called.

"Come here," they would say to Anthony.

Anthony would not comply. They would stand up and go to Anthony, kneel down, and say in a stern, clear voice, "I said come here," and then proceed to take Anthony gently by the hand and walk him over to where they had been standing when they gave the first "come here" command.

They would verbally reinforce Anthony and say, "Nice job coming here," and then pat him on the head and lead him away. He would go back to whatever toy, puzzle, or game he was tinkering with at the time the command was given.

Approximately two seconds later, they would call him again. If Anthony did not come, they would repeat the entire process. The process would be repeated over and over again hourly, daily, and monthly until he would come when he was called the first time. This "come here" directive would be practiced first in small areas (i.e., from one side of the room to the other side.) Then once Anthony was successful, we lengthened the space. "Come here" would be practiced from one room to the next. Once he mastered that, we proceeded to try it vertically, speaking from upstairs to downstairs. It took months of hard work to get Anthony to learn to "come here." Do you know how much more there is to teach in life than that simple direction to "come here?" The therapists were ruthless, and they kept persisting. They did not give up. It was like training a stallion or perhaps breaking one in, I'm not sure which. Anthony did not want to come when called. It was far easier when Mom came to him.

Consistency was the key to teaching Anthony new skills. The therapists would make sure Anthony mastered a specific skill in all areas, which they called generalization, before moving onto the next developmental mark. Generalization is a term that referred to Anthony generalizing or being able to demonstrate that he understood that directive in every environment. For Anthony to have a skill mastered, he would need to demonstrate success with at least three different therapists in at least three different environments. His environment could be school, home, or a playground. It wasn't uncommon for Anthony to demonstrate the understanding of a concept at home, but when placed in an unfamiliar environment, he may not be able to demonstrate knowledge or application of that same skill. Generalization was a key component to Anthony's overall success and progress.

Tantrums, throwing items, hitting, punching, kicking, screaming, wetting himself, and spitting were only a few of the behaviors brought out when we were teaching him to comply. The therapists' thoroughness, consistency, and "don't give an inch" attitude got us through those difficult times. The key was also teaching me that my hours with Anthony were vital to his success. I couldn't rely on the few hours each day they were with him to be enough to move his progress. Real success is ... therapy around the clock with every person who dealt with my son. I had to be his therapist and his mom as well as teach every person who interacted with him the skills I had learned from the therapists. For him to be successful and progress, I had to pick up the slack and the skills of consistency around the clock with my son. Therapy wasn't only for him. It was for me. They taught me that I was his greatest therapist. They would only be in his life for a short period of time. I would be in his life for as long as the Lord would allow.

I firmly believe God places every person in our lives for a reason. Perhaps it's for them, perhaps for us, or perhaps for both, but it's not a coincidence. ABA therapists were placed in our lives to show me that my son could learn. He could behave. He could listen. He may not be like everybody else or learn every skill in the universe, but he had the capability. ABA brought hope and light to my darkness and skepticism. They didn't only teach my kid. They taught me, which in my eyes was instrumental in helping Anthony. It's like when you get in an airplane and that pleasant flight attendant tells you to first secure your oxygen mask before helping your child. They secured my mask and showed me how to secure Anthony's.

Today Anthony comes to me from wherever he is and from whatever he is doing when I call, and he says "What, Mom?" He has even learned to say, "May I finish what I am doing?" or, "I need a second."

I thank Jesus for allowing the right people to be placed on Anthony's path ... and on mine. I also thank Him for allowing me to acknowledge those things.

Chapter 7 Review

This is your takeaway …

- Your child will change his or her behavior when you change yours.
- Praise the good and *extinguish* the bad.
- Be consistent in your expectations everywhere you go and every time you speak.
- *Never give up!*

  Look, you scoffers, wonder and perish, for I am going to do something in your days that you would never believe, even if someone told you.

  —Acts 13:41

Chapter 8

THE SEVENTH DAY

Thus the heavens and all the earth were completed in all their vast array. By the seventh day God had finished the work he had been doing; so on the seventh day he rested from all his work. Then God blessed the seventh day and made it holy, because on it he rested from all the work of creating that he had done.

—Genesis 2:1–3

How do you take a day off of parenting? What does that even look like? "Not now, kids. Deal with your own issues. Mom's taking a break. Go figure it out on your own." Perhaps those statements work well when you have teenagers and are trying to develop some independence and self-responsibility. However, when you have small toddlers and one with a disability, who can find the time to relax? Rejuvenate? Unwind? Well, I didn't make any time. I didn't squeeze much "Debbie time" into Anthony's speech time, OT time, or behavioral time. That was a fatal mistake. Our heavenly Father, God Almighty, even takes time. An entire day!

I don't know if I was living in Martyrville or so consumed with caring for my son. I guess it doesn't really matter which. I do know now that I ignored my friends' and family's plea to unwind and relax. They would often tell me that I needed to stop and take care of myself, that I was doing too much for others. They all told me that I would burn out.

I ignored them.

I burned out.

The reason I share this with you is because it may be hard for some of us to give ourselves permission to relax both physically and mentally. Relaxing physically is an arduous task for me. I am active, and I am constantly in motion. It seems like I live in my car some days because I'm always driving somebody somewhere. To stop and sit seems to be such a waste of time when I can be doing something productive like checking something off my list so that I don't have to do it later. I have learned, though, that sitting is active—not in the sense of exercise but in the sense of actively choosing to rest your body. When I rest my body, I feel better. It's not a waste of time. It's time well utilized when I do it in moderation. To really stop and smell the roses ... or even to see that somebody planted them is good. It's nice to slow down. It's essential.

Relaxing mentally is also an arduous task. To shut my brain off from worrying and feeling guilty that "I may not be doing enough for my family" is just plain tough. I once heard that worrying is concentrating too much on the future and feeling guilty is living in the past, neither of which is productive! Living in the present, the here and now, is truly all we have to do. In fact, when I can stop looking in the past and focusing on the future, then I really am living in the present, which is another gift. I have to force myself to relax both physically and mentally. When I do, then I'm really living in the moment. And that's all we are really supposed to do anyway, right? "Therefore do not *worry* about *tomorrow*, for *tomorrow* will *worry* about itself. Each day *has* enough trouble of its own" (Matthew 6: 34).

I believe it's equally hard for both stay-at-home parents as well as working parents. I know. I have been both. As a stay-at-home mom, I was *on* the entire day. When the kids would go to bed, my mind would be *on* with reading research and scrambling around the Internet for help for my boy. I never shut off or unplugged my brain. I never gave myself permission to relax, let go of the stress, and simply *be*. I was afraid I would be wasting valuable time finding out how to help my son overcome autism.

According to many new studies and Gallup polls, stay-at-home moms may be more depressed, angry, and emotionally unsettled than their counterparts. Many studies reveal that it could be the financial strain put on the families, the worry and anxiety that accompanies parenting, or the lack of appreciation felt daily. Nevertheless, the amount of pressure that may be experienced by stay-at-home moms can be relieved if they make time for themselves and their needs. Parenting is a full-time job whether you are physically with your child or not. You can ease the stress by indulging in time away physically and mentally and filling that time with things that make you feel happy and confident.

It's definitely not any easier for a working parent. When I was working as an administrator as well as a teacher, I continued to be *on* all day only to come home feeling guilty for not being with my children during the day and remain on my "A" game for the entire evening. If you are a working parent, you may have experience with those same feelings. It was exhausting. I wasn't doing anybody any favors walking through life exhausted, especially me. If you search the Internet for statistics related to the amount of stress working moms have, it's staggering. Most studies point to the fact that working parents feel extremely stressed out, anxious, and even depressed. Many fill their nights and weekends with work and feel that they will eventually burn out. In addition, many feel exhausted and guilty, that whatever they do is just not enough. I've been there too.

It's okay to take time and rejuvenate our souls. If we choose to do it spiritually, we are filled with His strength and His stamina.

We don't have to do it alone. I spend time each morning thanking our Lord for all He has given me. I spend time in His Word and in His promises. I thank Him throughout the day for everything, including any challenges I may be facing. Because He is good and I know He loves me, it's easier to rest in *all* that He gives me. Even when that *all* includes challenges. In every challenge there lays an opportunity—an opportunity to grow and learn to overcome. I believe He allows challenges in our lives to shape us into the people He has created us to be. Sometimes we can only learn those things through the obstacles in which He allows.

Rejuvenating our souls looks different for everybody. I have experienced rejuvenation when I go to the gym or run in our hills because it releases my stress, physically speaking. I have also learned to read for pleasure and not always for research. I find it relaxing to cook our favorite meals and to collect new recipes for family and friends. I like to meet up with my girlfriends and enjoy sharing in their lives and in their journeys. I have joined a small group of women at my church, and I have made many new friends and spiritually grown with their wisdom. I have also found that I enjoy writing a book to encourage and inspire others.

What do you enjoy doing? Reading, cooking, running … or perhaps traveling, hiking, and fishing? Find your passion or develop one. Cultivate your soul and give yourself permission to revitalize your own life. Everybody you encounter will thank you.

Detaching from your challenges one day a week is a gift God knew we needed. I rest today. I do not feel guilty when I rest. I am better for my children, my husband, and everybody else. I am better for me. I'm still a work in progress when it comes to the idea of *total* rest for an entire day. That continues to be a struggle for me. But when I read my Father's instructions, it helps. His perspective is higher than mine. And if Chick-fil-A, Hobby Lobby, and God can rest, then so can I. And so can you.

Chapter 8 Review

This is your takeaway ...

- Take care of yourself physically and emotionally.
- Don't feel guilty.
- Refresh your mind, body, and soul.
- *Never give up!*

Then the Lord said to Moses, "Say to the Israelites,
'You must observe my Sabbaths. This will be a sign
between me and you for the generations to come, so you
may know that I am the Lord, who makes you holy.'"

—Exodus 31:12–13

Chapter 9

OCEAN EYES

Independent, beautiful, strong, and tenacious, my daughter Allison is my "ocean eyes."

I am aware of the amount of time, energy, and attention devoted to my autistic son. I am also acutely aware of my daughter watching from the sidelines. Of course, I would try to make special mommy-daughter time, including manicures and pedicures, daily devotions at bedtime, and play dates with her girlfriends, in order to experience normal relationships with her. However, I have always feared that the mommy time is unfairly divided.

Allison Rose Dilley, my firstborn child, was blessed with beautiful blonde hair, porcelain skin, and ocean blue eyes. Ally, we affectionately call her, came into this world about twenty-one months sooner than her brother did. God really knew what He was doing when He placed Ally on this earth before her younger brother. Ally has truly been a gift in my life and in her brother's. I trust that your own family dynamics are just that, your own. However, I would like to share some insights from my Ocean Eyes that might shed some light on possible frustrations your other children may be feeling from time to time. I also hope you see some gifts they may receive simultaneously.

Having an autistic brother as a sibling brings challenges to the plate for Allison. The simple arguments and disagreements between siblings didn't occur early in their relationship because Anthony didn't speak, let alone argue and disagree. The typical competitions and games that kids learn from didn't happen because Anthony didn't care about competing for anything. She didn't experience fun game nights because Anthony didn't know how to play board games. In fact, a lot of typical life was missing for my Ocean Eyes as she grew up in a special family.

In place of these typical family activities, Allison encountered family invasions. Therapists entered our home daily and put a new spin on Allison's view of what typical life looked like. She lived with the notion that people come to our home each day to spend hours teaching her little brother skills. Although they included her whenever and wherever possible, their main focus was Ally's brother, not Ally. I'm not sure how that would feel. I am not sure how one would view this world, looking through the very consistent lens "My brother seems to be more special than me. Look at all of the attention he gets. Look at the attention I don't get."

Many therapists did enter our homes. Our lives. Our family. It was almost always about Anthony, and I consistently was concerned about Ally. As any parent would be. When I spoke to her about this, she agreed she felt that Anthony was the main attraction. She noticed the attention he received, but her first response was as follows:

It didn't matter—

I didn't care about it—

However, when pressing harder I got more of her heart. She expressed to me that it was hard to see the therapist's play and help him. She felt it when they couldn't or wouldn't incorporate her. She felt like she was more on the inside looking out. However, she told herself the following:

It doesn't matter—

He needs the help—

I understand—

I believe Ally used these phrases to help cope with the isolation she must have felt. Although some say it's the autistic child who is in isolation, I often wonder if it's the siblings who may feel like that. I questioned who really was isolated in those days in our home—the child with autism or the child without. That is something to grapple with.

I asked Ally to explain in her own words what it has been like growing up with an autistic brother. Without any prompting, coaching, or aiding her, this is what my nine-year old daughter wrote:

Dear Readers,
As you know my
fabulus mom has been working
so hard on helping other people.
She is the best mom you can
get. With Anthony you need
a lot of patcuts. Sometimes
Anthony gets on my nearves,
just like any brother? See
with an oddisfic kid you need:
Patunts, Love, Time. Every kid in
the world needs thouse things,
if they don't get them who knows
what will happen. Anthony is
the best thing that happened
to me and my family. Some kids
are mean to kids with disablitys,
I just don't undrostand why
you would be so mean.
Anthony is great at
many things asplayly playing mare.
Brothere and dooing math. He neede
help with reading comporation. We
all struggle in things, like
I struggle in math, but I am
ok with getting help. And you
should be ok with getting help to.
Anthony has gotten so
far! Belive me when I say that.
I Have fun reading the
rest of the book!

As I read her letter, I see that she gives praise to me and she gives love to him. That is very typical of Ally, never wallowing in a "poor me" attitude. She notices the hard work it takes to raise kids when she's a child herself. She witnesses how others treat her brother and the injustices of that behavior. She acknowledges her little brother's annoying behavior from to time to time and seems to be completely accepting. She has consistently displayed an enormous amount of patience for this lifestyle in our home. This is the only lifestyle she has known, and it is sculpting her into the beautiful person she is becoming.

I have used the letter she wrote many years ago when I first began writing my book as a tool to help me draw out more of Ally's heart. She was nine at the time, and after many revisions of this book and years later, I went back and chatted with her. She was very eager to cooperate. I began asking her to explain the patience or "patents" thing she wrote about in her letter and what that exactly meant to her. She responded with statements such as:

"He agitates me with his constant talking to himself. It's annoying and irritating." (Anthony used to talk to himself in jargon and nonsense. Therapists referred to this as a verbal self-stimulatory behavior. They believed he did this as a self-soothing technique to calm himself down.)

"His behaviors are embarrassing for me. Everybody always looks at us, and it makes me uncomfortable." (Those behaviors were his tantrums in public or his constant need for redirection from me. They were embarrassing for a typical kid trying not to stand out in a crowd.)

"He repeats himself and ruminates on the same topic over and over again. We have to constantly repeat ourselves with him about everything. It's tiring. He doesn't get it the first time. He needs to be told over and over again. He needs to be validated many times before it sinks in his head. It's constant. It gets old." (I cannot really say anything to this one because her observation is spot on. I do need to constantly repeat myself with him. He does seem to learn best with repetition and consistency. It does get old. It is constant. I get it.)

After she shared these irritations with me, I wondered where the patience thing came in. "All of this patience" she professed then were missing in her examples. She then told me that "all of this patience" she has learned from Anthony hasn't always been *given* to Anthony. She feels that she has learned to be more patient *with others* because of Anthony.

Patient with other people's habits.

Patient with other people's challenges.

Patient with other people's delays.

Patient with other people's irritating comments and behaviors.

She tries to be patient with her brother, but as life has it, he is still a brother. I guess there was sibling rivalry present that I didn't always observe.

The part of her letter discussing "people who are mean to Anthony" broke my heart. I asked her how others interact with her brother, and she shared two important rays of light on the topic. First, she has learned how to speak up and stand up for herself and others, including her brother, because of him. She has learned she has a voice and how to speak her mind when he didn't have a voice and he couldn't share his thoughts. She feels strongly that this skill is a gift given to her because of him. Secondly, she is often irritated that others treat him differently because of his disability. She wants others to treat him the same as any other kid because he is a typical kid in her eyes.

"If people treat him special, then he acts in a more manipulative way. He needs discipline and boundaries like everybody else. Yeah, he has some needs, but the expectations people have of him are too low. They baby him too much. He can do much more than people give him credit for. People should treat him as if he didn't have those challenges, and then he won't have them as much."

Expect the moon and land in the stars. Expect the side of the barn, and you will land in the mud. She prefers expecting the moon. I think she gets some of that from her mother.

Today she is a teenager. In those short years of life, I have watched her develop patience because she needed to slow down before she spoke. She has also had to learn how to wait until he understands a concept, and perhaps learn how to teach it to him in a different way. I have also seen her develop grace because she has had to learn to forgive him for the many adversities she has had to experience. Forgiving is such an important character trait that so many of us struggle with, and learning and practicing this at a young age is a gift.

I've recognized that she has learned there is a time for everything, even when she didn't know she needed to learn that. Timing is such an important skill to learn. Learning the time to talk, walk away, teach, learn, leave, and stay are vital aspects of good relationships. She has had to learn there is a time for her and a time for him. She had to learn this a little differently than the rest of us had to since her brother, who has a disability, requires a lot of time on everybody's part.

She has witnessed and experienced kindness in so many different ways from so many different people on earth. She has continuously witnessed therapists and doctors being patient and kind with him. She grew up with people trying to include her in his programs and therapies. Kindness isn't always easy to observe within people. Ally has been blessed to experience that character trait with many.

She saw that everybody, including herself, had their needs met, and this taught her how to trust. To trust that we are safe and that we are exactly where we are supposed to be is more than a gift. It's a token of God's love, a tribute. Trusting is something we volunteer to do without force. Learning to trust may also be a lifelong journey. I am grateful she has learned that from an early age.

As a young adolescent, Ally already knows how to speak her mind and has taught Anthony to do the same. She has learned how to help others see how to understand him and how he best learns. She has taught him how to socially fit in and how to behave in public. She has taken on the job of always keeping an eye on him and helping him see the world as she does. She shared with me that she feels she is a more loving person because of Anthony. I didn't understand what she meant by that, so I asked her to explain.

"He has such a huge heart, Mom. How can't people love more when they see him love? He loves so much, and he doesn't hold back. He doesn't play games. He only loves. It's true, and it's real. He doesn't care what he looks like. When he wants to hug, he hugs. When he wants to say he loves you, he says he loves you. He doesn't look around to see who is watching. He doesn't care who is watching. He just loves. He loves with his entire heart. I feel I'm more loving because of Anthony, Mom."

Patience, grace, timing, nurturing, trusting, communicating, and love—what incredible things to learn when you are young! These incredible traits make her more beautiful than her amazing physical traits of blonde hair, olive skin, and amazing ocean eyes!

Now don't get me wrong. The sibling rivalry is alive and well in our home. We have game nights, movie nights, and typical family events. We discuss, argue, and disagree exactly like other families would experience. We actually seem somewhat typical to the naked eye. Most of my friends tell me they pull their hair out when their children fight, argue, and whine with one another. They share that it's unbearable and miserable, and they feel that it tears the family apart. I smile and say, "Mine argue and fight too. Isn't it fabulous?"

So many wonderful things occur when we trust we are exactly where we need to be. The peace is unsurpassed if we trust and believe things work for the good for the lives of those who love the Lord. Trusting God in all times and circumstances has been the cornerstones of the true peace I have encountered on this earth. When I begin taking back my trust and controlling it myself, things go awry. I am indebted to Him for allowing my daughter to experience trust, grace, and forgiveness at such a tender age. I'm indebted to my dear friend as well for advising me to explore my daughter's heart and include her words and feelings in this chapter.

Because of my belief that we are exactly where we need to be in life, I feel safe that Allison is where she needs to be as much as Anthony is. I trust she is learning what she needs to in her life and on her journey and that God will take care of her exactly as He takes care of her brother. I trust she will become the whole woman she is meant to be because of her experiences within her home, and I believe that she can perhaps even help other siblings who have experienced similar journeys.

Chapter 9 Review

This is your takeaway …

- All children are gifts from God.
- Special siblings have special siblings.
- Carve out alone time with your other children. They will cherish it.
- *Never give up!*

> *And my God will meet all your needs according to the riches of his glory in Christ Jesus.*
>
> *—Philippians 4:19*

> *And we know that in all things God works for the good of those who love him, who have been called according to his purpose.*
>
> *—Romans 8:28*

> *People were also bringing babies to Jesus for him to place his hands on them. When the disciples saw this, they rebuked them. But Jesus called the children to him and said, "Let the little children come to me, and do not hinder them, for the kingdom of God belongs to such as these."*
>
> *—Luke 18:15–16*

Chapter 10

UNITED WE STAND ...
DIVIDED WE FALL

Do families with autistic children have a greater chance of divorce than those without? I researched many different resources and was unable to find an accurate answer to this question. Most research does revolve around the idea that if families can get through the first few years of the child's disability, then the likelihood of staying together increases. The research was unclear and indecisive, though, about the actual statistics of divorce rates among families with disabilities. I guess it is a rather moot point now. I became a statistic. Hopefully, I can share some of my "aha" moments and possibly help another family stay together.

I do not claim to understand how intimate relationships work among people, and I haven't had such an incredible track record in that area. Since my divorce, I have read as many books on relationships as I have on autism. If I would have read a few of them during my marriage, I may have been able to better deal with our conflicts. One book that really stands out for me today is *Marriage Builders* by Larry Crabb. This book really takes a Christian perspective on looking at one's own manipulations and motivations and how each person brings those manipulations into their marriage. It is an excellent resource that I read a bit late. I guess it's never really too late to learn and grow and pass that knowledge onto my daughter. I've learned to take that hard look in the mirror not only with my parenting but with my intimate relationships as well. I am finding that's another really hard look to take. Divorce will do that to you. It hasn't been an inviting process, but it sure has been an enlightening one.

We met at Taco Bell. I was a busy girl at age sixteen, going to school and working a part-time job. I was proud to wear those polyester uniforms and earn an honest dollar. I was enjoying balancing my job and my schoolwork simultaneously. I clearly remember the day he walked in. A tall, handsome, blonde athlete strolled in with his friends. He ordered two bean burritos with no onions and a large Pepsi. That was it! I was cooked. We married nine years later. He was my high school sweetheart, my hero, my ... everything! We were in love. Love was enough at sixteen, right? That is what so many kids believe at that tender age. Love will be enough.

After about four years of marriage, we hoped to begin our family. With the grace of God, we were given Allison Rose Dilley—a beautiful, blonde-haired, blue-eyed, porcelain skin baby girl. Our daughter became everything to us. I was able to take about six months off of my busy assistant principalship to care for her before returning to work. We loved spending time with our tenacious, precious girl. She was smart, funny, outgoing, talkative, and inquisitive. She followed me around and pretended she was an adult from an early age. She was a bit stubborn at times, but I chalked that up to a normal toddler.

Twenty-one months later, God blessed us again, this time with a little boy. Anthony James Dilley came silently into the world at seven pounds, eleven ounces. He was the polar opposite of his sister, both in physical appearance as well as in personality attributes. He entered the world with dark brown hair, chocolate-brown eyes, and perfectly tanned, olive skin. He was handsome. His personality wasn't like his sister's. He wasn't talkative or funny. He rarely followed me around and hardly ever attempted to mimic what his father or I did. Role-playing and pretending did not happen.

Allison loved her new baby brother. She was the perfect older sister, helping her parents and doting over our new addition to the family. She loved being the older sister and took charge of her new baby brother as if he were a toy. She handed him everything, and he wanted for nothing. In fact, as the months passed and his silence continued, we attributed some of his *delayed* development to his overanxious and helpful parents, his sister, and other family members. I remember some family members telling me there would be no reason for him to talk when we were doing everything for him. My pediatrician even said, "Oh, it's common for second kids to be a bit slower. Second children have a lot done for them, so they don't have to talk. You're such a busy mom with two kids, work, a husband, and a house. It's no wonder you do for him. It's easier than teaching him to do for himself." Oh, how I remember those burning words.

Nevertheless, the dad was very proud of his son. He now had his beautiful girl and handsome boy and the big house. What more could one ask for?

Well, life didn't quite progress the way we thought it would. He had a perfect house, a perfect wife (as I would like to think), kids, jobs, cars, and those things that are supposed to bring happiness to a young couple. But as days turned to weeks and weeks turned to months, Anthony's silence remained. Pediatrician visits were more frequent. Speech therapy began. Occupational therapy started. Behaviorists came into our house daily to teach us how to parent our silent boy and his tantrums.

Diagnosis ... autism. Now what? As that diagnosis finally sunk in, I should have explored counseling, therapy, or other means of support for my marriage. I remember having a conversation with Tony at the time, sharing with him that I had read the divorce rate of parents with autistic children was 85 percent. The normal divorce rate was 50 percent at the time. I expressed my fear to him that I didn't want to wind up being a statistic. He told me not to worry.

I didn't seek other support measures and jumped into my son's diagnosis with two feet. I handled most of the situation alone. I studied and read constantly. I was researching therapies until midnight most nights. I advocated for our son at meetings and dealt with numerous doctors and specialists. I took him to all of his doctor appointments and therapies, and I quit my job. I learned a new way to parent. I turned my house upside down for his behavior therapy and became my son's therapist as well as his mother.

I had specialists in my home more than forty hours a week, telling me how to help my son learn and grow. I tried to be a good wife and also a half-sane parent to Allison. It was extremely difficult and challenging. I didn't often make time for my own needs, which I see today, regretfully. And that is where chapter 8 was born. If I would have taken care of me somewhere down that challenging path, I might not have given up. I ran out of everything one needs in order to have a healthy marriage. I ran empty on patience, understanding, and forgiveness. Instead of those healthy, loving qualities, other emotions filled my heart. Resentment, anger, and loneliness were strong emotions I allowed to fester and to grow. I let them into my heart and allowed them to take up residence.

I remember leaning on my husband for emotional support because I was drowning in a sea of worry, paperwork, doctors, therapies, and a host of other issues. I would often call him several times at work to hear his voice and stay grounded in our love. I was met with him saying, "I can't talk right now. I can't deal with this right now. I am working." I vividly remember our marriage counselor sharing with Tony that I was seeking some solid ground to stand on instead of my quicksand, and he was that solid ground for me. He would counter, "I can't deal with her and work at the same time." She advised me to call him once a day and write down anything else I wanted to talk about and share with him later.

I felt so alone. With all of the chaos around me, I felt so very alone.

Looking back, I should have also leaned on my faith, the only substance that is everlasting and always present. But I did not. I prayed, of course, but not with the vigor I pray with today. Nevertheless, I am convinced the sea of worry didn't just fall in only my boat. I'm pretty certain Anthony's father experienced it too. After all, this was his son as well. This was his shining star that was supposed to follow in his dad's footsteps and run down the football field with that little brown ball. Anthony was his future. But I could not see, taste, or feel any of those things because I was drowning in my own self-imposed worry. I was exhausted and emotionally drained. I was allowing negative emotions and thoughts to fill my heart instead of the hope and strength that only comes from the Lord.

I have learned so many things about relationships. I've learned communication is extremely important and you must say how you feel and what you think. I am learning that stuffing those feelings under the rug doesn't really make them go away. They really do come out on the other side so much dirtier than when you originally stuffed them under in the first place. I've learned that the core values people share must be pretty close to being exactly the same, and that the core values of a person do not change … ever. Hence, you must really be able to accept them initially. Most importantly, I've learned that respect is vital and should be given consistently and regularly by both people.

Respect is a little word that means so very much in relationships. It is the glue that holds marriages together in difficult times, and it's the light in all situations. Respect can sometimes take the form of *acceptance* of one another's differences and opinions. I didn't really accept his differences respectfully. I often bulldozed him into agreeing with mine. I remember so many times I had to be right about issues, and guess what? The only way to be right is if somebody else (usually him) is wrong. I would even cite evidence to prove my opinions were correct and use therapists and doctors' words to prove my case. I think I missed my calling as a lawyer. I cannot speak for him, but it really can't feel that great to always be on the defense, where I kept him so often. Although he played defense in college football, I'm confident enough to say he probably didn't want to play defense in our marriage.

Respect can also take the form of *allowance* for one another's own journeys and timing. I wasn't too good with this one either. I often disrespected Tony's journey in life and his timing with accepting Anthony's diagnosis. I wanted and yearned for him to be on my page so that we could jointly help our family. Looking back, I didn't see that his journey was separate from mine. We were different people, traveling our own personal journeys under the same roof. I didn't do so well accepting that fact or even really acknowledging it. Again, the purpose of sharing my personal story with you is to introduce an awareness of your own journey. I am not saying you are living in the dark. I am sharing that I was. I have learned to accept those darker days, as they were part of my journey. If I hadn't walked through some darkness, I wouldn't have known where the light started.

Respect is not a destination you arrive at by doing it well once. It is a verb that requires daily actions and behaviors on the part of each person. It is in the smiles, the words, the energy, and the behaviors portrayed to people every time you speak and interact with them. It's in every choice I make every day. It's a lot more than seven letters. It's the foundation of a healthy relationship, and without it, *it* becomes the demise of one.

I have also learned that every day is a gift, and sometimes I took those days for granted. I am also acutely aware we all have choices about how we are going to treat one another and that those choices add up like a score card, whether we want them to or not. The good choices somehow seem to get overlooked, however, while the bad choices are hard to erase because they are usually written in ink on our hearts. Consistency is key to relationships as well as to parenting. Parents have to stand together as a team in raising their children. If perhaps they do not agree or feel the same way, they need to discuss those issues out of the earshot of those children and with a respectful tongue. There's that *respect* thing again.

We were not united on many fronts. I liked to parent with clear boundaries and rewards. Tony had a more relaxed and comfortable approach. We were raised very differently, which always had a huge effect on how we wanted to raise our children. A strict disciplinarian mother and father raised me. It was what some people would coin "old school."

"Do what you're told the first time."

"Kids should be seen and not heard."

"I am the parent, and you are the child."

"That is what is for dinner. Eat it, or you'll be hungry."

"Because I said so—that's why!"

Tony did not have the same upbringing. Eventually, those core values clashed. In fact, they didn't only clash. They were at the center of every disagreement and argument in our home.

When we began therapy and strict boundaries and consequences were placed on Anthony, the light shone on how very different our core values really were. It seemed to be extremely difficult for Tony to deal with our son's tantrums. I would do almost every bit of therapy, and Tony rarely participated. He made it very clear he found it too difficult to discipline Anthony even when he was acting out. I vividly remember a huge, three-hour tantrum in our living room with one of Anthony's therapists, Anthony, and me. It started over Anthony hitting me because he didn't want to put his shoes on and go for a walk. The behavior strategy used during this episode was coined "overcorrection." The goal of overcorrection was to make Anthony realize if he made a poor choice, such as hitting in this case, he would have to hit a pillow excessively until he didn't want to hit anymore. Hopefully, he would hit the pillow so many times he would exhaust his desire to hit that pillow, me, and everyone else. Hence, the term overcorrecting. You would overcorrect the problem at hand and hopefully deter it from arising again. Well, as one can imagine, he didn't want to hit the pillow. He didn't want to follow any adult directives. The tantrum continued. The yelling got louder. This behavior intervention was difficult. Tony, our daughter, and I were sitting at the kitchen table while the therapist was overcorrecting Anthony. I asked Tony to go in and watch so that when the therapist left, he would know how to deal with his son. I always encouraged him to learn how to deal with Anthony's behaviors and be involved in the therapy process. I clearly remember his response. "I can't," he said. "It's too much for me."

The light was beaming brightly on how truly divided we really were. You see, it was too much for me as well, but someone had to do it. It was extremely difficult to walk those roads alone. I remember how lonely they were. There was much resentment built because of those lonely roads. Resentment turns to anger and bitterness. They are poison for relationships. I couldn't inspire, teach, wish, hope, or want enough for Tony to get involved and help carry the load. What's that great ol' saying? You can bring a horse to water, but you can't make him drink. Yes, I couldn't make him drink in the therapy, drink in the philosophy, or drink in the reality of our life. I couldn't make him want to learn the skills and tools of the therapy sessions. I couldn't make it easier on him. We were divided. We were divided on many fronts. "United we stand. Divided we fall." We fell. We fell hard.

Looking in the rearview mirror, I see that it wasn't my job to make him accept our reality. It wasn't my place or my duty. It also wasn't my job to change him in any way. My duty was to help our son and pray for our family. My job was to tend to the family and respect my husband. "She brings him good, not harm, all the days of her life" (Proverbs 31:12).

My job was to keep my mind on all things that were good. It was to keep my thoughts and my behaviors positive and uplifting to those around me. It was to see the good in our differences and not the negative. It was to choose my battles carefully, not to focus on them consistently. It was to honor my husband. "Finally, brothers and sisters, whatever is true, whatever is noble, whatever is right, whatever is pure, whatever is lovely, whatever is admirable-if anything is excellent or praiseworthy-think about such things" (Philippians 4:8).

Finally, my job was to respect my husband. It was to accept his journey and his timing. It was to allow him to be him without my interference. It was to respect him and his walk on this earth, although it wasn't the same as mine. It was never supposed to be the same as mine.

Since our divorce, Tony has had both of our kids alone and without me around. He has had to become a more involved parent because I'm not there on a daily basis helping him with it. He has had to figure out the best ways to help both of his children. He has learned. He has grown.

I saw my journey through my glasses only, and I see life through a different lens today. I have learned many things along this road. I have learned that going through a diagnosis of a disabled child is challenging for everyone, not just me. I have learned his parenting style was different than mine—not a wrong approach, a different one. I have learned that pride was a problem for me, and I continue to struggle with it from time to time. I learned I was judgmental, and that isn't easy to live with either. I am growing, though not of my own accord. I am learning about my pride through reading the one book I should have been reading all along, the Bible. The Bible teaches the things one needs to know, including how to be a good wife and how to parent children. Not really a coincidence. The book of Proverbs is the place to read about parenting children, if one wishes to receive wisdom in that area of life. The book of Proverbs also shares an entire chapter on "The Wife of Noble Character."

The reason I write this chapter is to share that any time a family is faced with a challenge of any magnitude, whether it is an illness, a medical diagnosis, or a development disability, it would be wise to seek support together as a family. As I was chasing my husband for emotional support, he was fleeing from it all. It was a lot of pressure and stress placed on our family. When anyone or anything is chased, I've learned they run. I should have been chasing my faith. Today I do. The strength and hope are amazing and enough. He is enough.

I can only share with you a mother's perspective regarding this diagnosis and an ex-wives perspective on a failed marriage. At the advice of few good friends, I asked Tony if he would consider sharing what he has learned through the diagnosis of his son, what advice he would give to other dads who might be in his shoes.

He graciously agreed to share his message.

As statistics for divorce continue to increase with special needs families, my plea to all of the dads out there is to ask themselves two questions.

1. Do you love your family?
2. Are your children the most important things your life?

I'm sure 99.9 percent of fathers said yes to both of those questions. With that said, here is my message to you:

1. Don't run to your *cave*. No explanation needed for men.
2. Make it a priority to *educate* yourself on *autism*.
3. Have a conversation or two with your spouse, and outline each of your expectations for the roles you will play in your *fight* against autism.

4. Play an *active* role in the plan (ABA therapy, IEPs, school meetings, etc.) that will help your child.
5. *You* are the *man* of the household. Be prepared for the *fight*.
    a. Fight to get your child's life back.
    b. Fight to keep your family together.
    c. Fight to keep your marriage healthy.
6. Get *professional* help, whether that be counseling, church groups, or support groups, *even* if you think you don't need it. (For those macho men out there, I'm speaking to you too!)

You are either about to begin or in the middle of the biggest fight of your life. I pray for each of you to engage, embrace, and train yourself for this venture. Don't follow in my footsteps and listen to your ego as I listened to mine. I don't want anybody else contributing to the divorce rate with special needs families. I want to leave you with one thought from Christopher Reeves, "Anyone can give up; it's the easiest thing in the world to do. But to hold it together when everyone else would understand if you fell apart, that's true strength." Find your strength and fight for your family and for your child.

—Tony

The one thing that remains very sad to me is that we had to fall to learn. We had to fail to see. We had to divorce to grow. We had to crumble before we rebuilt. The Lord is also very clear on divorce. The book of Malachi speaks very clearly to this. Scripture is full of light, and it is extremely clear if you seek it and let it sink into your soul.

Today we co-parent well. We both love our children very

much. We disagree on things relating to the children, but what family doesn't? We have learned to respect each other, and for the most part, we now think before we speak. We both have learned a lot from our son, our daughter, and our mistakes. Stay united on big issues, so you don't divide. Stay respectful of people's timing and journeys, and learn to accept people's thoughts and opinions that may differ from your own. Learn to let God.

United we stand.

Divided we fell.

Chapter 10 Review

This is your takeaway:

- Stay united on big issues.
- Get counseling or other support to help with conflict resolution.
- Respect each other's journeys.
- *Never give up!*

> *A gentle answer turns away wrath, but a harsh word stirs up anger.*
>
> —*Proverbs 15:1*

The Wife of Noble Character
Proverbs 31:10–31 (see appendix)

Chapter 11

A SECOND CHANCE

Did your marriage disintegrate? Do you wonder if you should walk that road again? I want to make my position very clear.

- I do not advocate divorce.
- I am not saying the grass is greener on the other side.
- I do not believe that if it's too hard, you should give up and look for something easier.

Although I do not wish the broken road on anybody's family, I do believe the Lord creates a beautiful canvas out of beautiful messes. I want to share part of my beautiful canvas with you now since you have seen my beautiful mess. It's amazing how despite my many flaws and mistakes, our heavenly Father weaves them together for the good to those who love Him. "And we know that in all things God works for the good of those who love him, who have been called according to His purpose" (Romans 8:28).

I have made many mistakes, and I am a flawed individual. But in all of that, I am truly forgiven. I have asked the Lord for forgiveness for my wrongdoings and my selfishness, and He has answered back with only grace, mercy, and forgiveness. He is transforming me, and He is shaping me into a new, better, and more pure person. It's His promise to me and to all who accept and know Him.

My son was five, and my daughter was turning seven when my divorce occurred. It was a dark season for our family. There were mistakes made and hard consequences to live with. If life could be painted on a canvas, ours would have had a picture of a cold, harsh, wintery forest. Trees would be barren and dormant while skies would be dark and gray. The soil would be layered with snow and mud, and a feeling of being chilled to the bones would be felt when scanning the canvas. As we prayed through those dark days and waded through the muck—literally and figuratively—my faith in the Lord grew stronger each day. I could see Him work in my life and my children's lives. I could see Him put some pieces together of a puzzle not yet completed.

As months and years passed, we all grew. The kids grew both physically and emotionally, and I grew spiritually. The fog seemed to lift. The gray days began to show signs of life and light. The heaviness began to dissipate. It's almost as if the season of life shifted from winter to spring. I saw the flowers bloom again, and the darkness faded to sunlight. I noticed birds chirping and dancing as if I had never known them to do that in all of my days. The laughter returned, and the hope for brighter times ahead increased.

Looking back, it was as if God prepared me for what was to come. I had not only read books about autism, but I also had read many books on relationships. I yearned to *grow* through my divorce and not *go* through it. In those books and even in the church classes on divorce care I attended, I learned a lot about how to take care of relationships and how to take care of people. I also learned that I might be open to trying it again someday. That was a very burdensome decision for me. To open myself up again emotionally and begin to trust in people and in love was difficult for me, and this time around I wouldn't be putting my own heart and hopes in a possible future relationship. I would also be putting my children's hearts and hopes into one as well. These were excruciating decisions to make.

Well, I didn't date much when I was young, and dating again in my thirties wasn't the most appealing thought. I started by going out with some of my girlfriends who were in the same boat. Into the single world we plunged, and sure enough, I didn't like it. I went on a few dates with a few men, but I found it extremely difficult to picture my life with any of them, especially when it came to seeing them as a stepdad to my children. I didn't introduce the children to any of them. I did not want to bring anybody home to meet the kids until I was sure it might go somewhere in the direction of a lasting relationship.

I did, however, meet one man in particular who did stand out. He was a friend of a friend, and he, too, had been recently divorced. We dated for a while. However, I wasn't comfortable introducing him to my kids. It was difficult because I really cared for him, but I didn't believe deep down he would be the right fit for us three or us three for him. Struggling with matching love interests is hard enough when you are alone. Combine that with two children, one with a disability, and it compounds the issue significantly.

After some time and a lot of prayer, I realized the Lord would bring me a man on His time, not on my time, if it was in His plan. So I continued to raise my kids and learn about myself. I continued growing, living, and learning. I was learning what made Debbie happy and how Debbie should live by putting the Lord first and asking for His discernment in my life. While this learning was taking place and when I wasn't looking for anybody to meet, the phone rang one evening. My longtime friend called me with plans of introducing me to a nice guy she thought would be perfect for me. I told her I wasn't sure. But knowing she knew what my family needed, I trusted her opinion, and she gave him my phone number. I spoke with him on the phone, and we seemed to connect well, so he asked me to join him for appetizers a few days later at a local restaurant.

When I met Rob, I was impressed with him on many levels. He was articulate, intelligent, well-traveled, and humorous. I liked him, but I was very cautious about giving my heart away too soon. We dated pretty consistently for about four months before I introduced him to the children. You can say I grilled him on every question one could possibly explore when dating. But as many people know, asking questions is only a piece of compiling the story. He needed to see my life, and I needed to see if he would be able to fit into it.

I had numerous conversations with Rob about Anthony's disability and how much effort, time, and work that challenge might bring. I was worried that Rob, a single man with no children, wouldn't want to jump into an established family with our special challenges. I tried to paint the canvas as clear and vivid as I could, but one has to live/see/breathe the life, not simply view the canvas to truly understand it. I also had many talks with Rob revolving around the sacrifices and effort it takes to raise children. Although Rob had been previously married and divorced, he had never fathered children. Rob had always longed to have his own children, but it didn't seem to be in God's plan. He always loved kids, and it was apparent by his early adult job choices. He had been a YMCA youth director at the young age of twenty-three. His job included driving fifty-five children between the ages of five and eight on a big yellow school bus. All of the children wanted to ride his bus because his was the "fun bus." (He made me write that.) Later in life he also took a mission trip with his church to Pisco, Peru. They delivered wheelchairs to the neediest patients in the outlying areas of the villages. They sang worship songs, shared the Lord with them, and provided kids and adults with much-needed transportation. What started out as a simple mission trip soon emerged as a disaster relief mission. The Pisco earthquake hit the same area at a magnitude of 7.9 when the church was doing their service. Rob and others helped in that disaster by digging trenches for village restrooms, building fences around the camps for safety, and packing and distributing care kits for families. As he shared these and other stories with me, I began to see his heart. As he revealed his heart, I began to fall in love with him. He is a good man. It seemed God had been preparing him for us as well. It seemed he had a journey to walk independent of ours to prepare his path for our journey together.

The day came when he met the kids. I was excited to share them with Rob and share Rob with them, but I was also nervous about the outcome. I didn't want to set anybody up for hope and futures if it wasn't going to work out, but I also knew that we'd have to move forward with the kids to see if there even *was* a hope and a future. I remember the day they met very well. Rob and I were going to go to a concert with another couple that evening. Prior to heading out on our date, I invited them all over to my house to meet the children. My family would also be there, babysitting. It was a full house with about fifteen people and some normal family chaos going on. Rob, his best friend, and his friend's wife came in, and I introduced them to Anthony and Allison for the first time. The kids were polite and probably thought nothing much of the introduction. Allison was about ten years old at the time, and Anthony was eight. They saw Mom head out with some friends to enjoy the night and wished us fun. I was terrified inside—terrified about what the kids were thinking, about what Rob was thinking, and even about what I was thinking. Instinctively terrified. But Rob was worth it for me to take step one. I very much cared for him, and I saw a future with him and with my kids.

Rob and his friends loved the kids. They interacted well and enjoyed the short visit with one another. So it was there the journey began. There were many family fun dates to the beach, movies, and the amusement parks. I wanted to observe Rob with the children in different kinds of environments. I gave him ample opportunities to see how family life would look, both during outside events and relaxing at home. He took on every challenge like a champ. He was patient, kind, and flexible. He differed to me on things he was unsure of and asked many questions. He really engaged with us, and the kids began to get as attached as I was.

I prayed earnestly in those early days, and the answers came down clear as crystal. "He says, 'Be still and know that I am God'" (Psalm 46:10**).**

I wanted anxiously to know if I was doing the right thing. I asked, "Was this the right man? Would the kids adapt? Would he stick around when it would get tough? Would Anthony's behaviors drive him crazy? Would a family in general be overwhelming?" The answer was always the same. "He says, 'Be still and know that I am God'" (Psalm 46:10). "Trust in the Lord with all your heart, and lean not on your own understanding; in all your ways submit to Him, and He will make your paths straight" (Proverbs 3:5–6).

So I took one day at a time and learned to wait. I learned to trust the Lord not only with my kids' futures but also with mine. Two years later we married and became a family. It became a *new* new for all of us. As we blended the different colors of sand on the beach together during our ceremony, we blended our lives. We blended our pasts in hopes for a future. We leaned on the Lord together as we learned how to navigate a blended family with special challenges. We also attended a twenty-week marriage-building class based on solid Bible principles in dealing with our marriage and ourselves.

Our story is young, but our lives are full and busy. Rob loves showing the kids and me the world. We travel often, and we see and experience new things. I recall one specific vacation after we got married when Rob took us to Maui, Hawaii. It was a grand vacation with its mix of typical family pandemonium. Rob wanted to take the kids to an authentic Hawaiian luau, swim with the turtles, and drive the very long road to Hana. As we experienced new adventures, we also experienced how we dealt with one another in conflict. In fact, when the pandemonium hit on the road to Hana after many miles of driving in the very compact rental car, Rob pulled over to take a minute, and he decided to walk the road to Hana. Anthony asked, "What is he doing?"

Ally replied, "He is taking a break from all of our arguing in the backseat." We laughed. We waited. We collected ourselves, and we stopped arguing.

Rob walked back and said, "Okay, I'm ready. Let's go!" We savored the rest of the day together, and we learned sometimes it's okay to take a break from one another, even if you have to walk the road to Hana for a bit and not drive it.

We grow in our love for one another because of the covenant we share, not the contract that we have. Marriage contracts can be dissolved. When the "my scorecard beats your scorecard" philosophy thrives, everybody loses. Rob works hard for all of us when he probably doesn't want to. That's love. We compromise for Rob when we don't want to. That's love too.

Rob also has been instrumental in helping me involve the kids in outside activities. We have the kids in activities in school such as color guard, track, swimming, and Boy Scouts. Rob takes Anthony on campouts with the Scouts and believes that hands-on life skills will be a lifelong benefit for him. He has helped provide structure and boundaries within our home with chores and the most consistent follow-through a parent can maintain. Coming from a very structured and strict house while growing up, Rob has brought much-needed structure to our home and our kids with patience and perseverance. Not only does he bring the structure Anthony needs, but he also mixes that with an amazing dose of fun and adventure. He has been perfect for our family, and I am blessed to have taken the second chance the Lord offered to me. It seems that God doesn't only have Anthony and Allison in His hands. He also is holding on to Rob and me.

I would offer the following tidbits of advice to anyone in my position:

- Take it slowly.
- Ask yourself if you are on the same page spiritually speaking or at least heading in the same direction.
- Ask a lot of questions, and don't worry about how that sounds to anybody else.
- Observe how your possible mate reacts in multiple situations over many different seasons of life.
- Really dig deeply and see if you can live with their flaws, and do not become consumed about them living with yours.

- Make sure there is mutual respect between the two of you from the very beginning of your courtship.
- Agree on who disciplines the children, and revisit that conversation if necessary.
- Ask yourself if the overall picture is brighter with him or her in your life.
- Observe if the children accept and respect him or her.
- Ask yourself if you ready for the emotional work it will take to walk this road again.
- Make sure your finances and children's futures are secure before blending lives legally.
- Seek the Lord's voice, and *be still* until you are sure it is His voice and not your hope.

These are a few questions and concerns that went through my head on the way down the aisle a second time. I didn't want to mess it up again. I had two children counting on me to do it right. I wanted to do what was pleasing to His kingdom and not mine. I truly hope these tidbits help you to seek what is best for you and your own family. If a second chance is what you desire and you are facing the challenges of single parenting, then I pray you will find it.

He is a big God.

A very big God.

Chapter 11 Review

This is your takeaway:

- Learn from your mistakes.
- Seek God in *all* of your decisions.
- Believe in faith, hope, and love.
- *Never give up!*

> *And now these three remain: faith, hope and love. But the greatest of these is love.*
>
> —*1 Corinthians 13:13*

Chapter 12

STUDENT IN TRAINING

I remember those paper dolls my sister and I used to play with, where you could magically attach the clothes to your doll and dress her in fashionable outfits. We would mix her blouses with different skirts and pants and create perfect little fashion divas. Then we would play with those other paper dolls—you remember, the annoying ones that had those cut out pieces of paper that you had to fold over the dolls body. I never really liked those paper dolls because the clothes would always be crooked and fall off. But nevertheless, we played with them and pretended to have a perfect life with them. We would have boy paper dolls, dog paper dolls, little kid paper dolls, and we would create perfect paper doll families. We eventually proceeded to the Barbie dolls with real clothes and accessories that didn't fall off. I loved those dolls. Everything fit like a glove, including her push-in earrings and jewelry, her hats, and those rubber shoes. Remember those rubber heels? It was so much fun living in a perfect pretend world.

Time passes, and we grow up, whether we are ready to or not. I received my two perfect children, neither of whom were like those pretend dolls. They were real little people with their own feelings, thought processes, behaviors, and beliefs. I was able to dress them the way I wanted like my Barbie dolls when I was growing up, but only for a short time. Then as they developed into their own little people, they began to have their own little opinions. I had to learn my job was to guide them with my value system and wisdom but allow them to develop into the people that God wanted them to be. What a daunting task to accomplish as a parent. Learning when to push them and learning when to allow them to learn on their own wasn't an easy order. I had a lot to learn.

I am not a medical doctor, psychologist, behavior therapist, or any other professional in terms of diagnosing or treating autism. Each and every person with this diagnosis may very well present with different symptoms. I am not claiming to *cure* or help kids *recover* in any way. I have attempted to share my experience with you from my perspective as a mother of a typical developing child and one who has autism. I have been there. I am still there. I will always be there. Was this diagnosis terrifying? Absolutely! Was I overwhelmed? *Yes* is an understatement. Did I face enormous challenges? Every day! Were there tears? Almost every night.

At the end of walking those roads, as challenging as they were, came many blessings. There is one song in particular I would hear on my Christian radio station that gripped my heart. It was a song that encompassed more than a melody and lyrics. It was as if the artist, Laura Story, was singing it right to me in the depths of my season of despair. The song is titled "Blessings", and I believe I was introduced to it at the exact moment I was supposed to hear it. Allow me to share the words with you, and perhaps the song can demonstrate that sometimes our blessings don't always come wrapped up like we would like them to.

Blessings
Laura Story (reprinted with permission)

We pray for blessings, we pray for peace
Comfort for family, protection while we sleep
We pray for healing, for prosperity

We pray for Your mighty hand to ease our suffering

All the while, You hear each spoken need
Yet love is way too much to give us lesser things

'Cause what if your blessings come through raindrops?
What if Your healing comes through tears?
What if a thousand sleepless nights
are what it takes to know You're near?

What if trials of this life
Are Your mercies in disguise?

We pray for wisdom, Your voice to hear
We cry in anger when we cannot feel You near
We doubt your goodness, we doubt your love
As if every promise from Your word is not enough

All the while, You hear each desperate plea
And long we'd have faith to believe

'Cause what if your blessings come through raindrops?
What if Your healing comes through tears?
And what if a thousand sleepless nights
are what it takes to know You're near?

And what if trials of this life
Are Your mercies in disguise?

When friends betray us, when darkness seems to win,
We know that pain reminds this heart
That this is not, this is not our home
It's not our home

'Cause what if your blessings come through raindrops?

What if Your healing comes through tears?
And what if a thousand sleepless nights
Are what it takes to know You're near?

What if my greatest disappointments
Or the aching of this life
Is the revealing of a greater thirst
this world can't satisfy?

What if trials of this life
The rain, the storms, the hardest nights...
Are Your mercies in disguise?

That song demonstrates beautifully that perhaps our blessings come in ways we cannot see so readily. Allow me to share some of my blessings with you.

With the challenge of the phone calls, the endless phone calls to different professionals to seek resources, wisdom, and answers in this diagnosis came the *blessing* of communicating more effectively with all types of people. I was able to really figure out how to get the answers I was seeking because I had so much practice with my many phone calls along the way.

Another challenge I faced was the countless doctor appointments, the speech services, and the occupational therapy appointments. The *blessing* that came from those countless appointments was recognizing I could seek several opinions and I didn't have to take the advice of one professional. I gained wisdom from each one. I also found there are many different professionals who are caring individuals, working earnestly at their jobs to help children like mine. I realized that so many people are truly gifts because they have chosen to help others who may be facing difficulties.

One massive mountain we faced as a family was having many different therapists in our home on a daily basis. If I stop to calculate that out so you can visualize what that would look like, it would read as followings:

- thirty hours a week for four years
- twenty-five hours a week for two years
- twenty hours a week for four years

That approximately totals 3,900 hours of in-home therapy over the course of Anthony's childhood. In other words, 234,000 minutes of people in my home, helping my son with basic skills and teaching him appropriate behaviors. That's a major invasion of family time everybody had to endure. The *blessing* I believed bestowed on me after all of those hours of in-home behavior therapy came in gifts of learning patience and persistence. I watched these individuals, often younger than me, be so patient with Anthony. It was spectacular. It didn't matter if it took thirty-five trials. They would press on and continue to try to teach my autistic son appropriate behaviors and actions so he could function in a more socially appropriate manner. I learned a lot of patience and perseverance in those 234,000 minutes of training. He wasn't the only one being trained. I was being trained as well.

Another time-consuming challenge was reading the numerous books and articles I had to consume to familiarize myself with autism. The *blessing* available for me, if I chose to view it that way, was the realization that there is a sea of help, information, and hope available for anybody searching to find it.

The constant, never-ending, tedious job of retraining my child's behaviors presented a constant challenge that I continue to face. The *blessing*, simply put, was that I learned all kids can learn if given ample opportunity, a lot of reinforcement, and a set of clear boundaries and consequences. Truly, it has been an endowment to be able to reach kids when they seem unreachable. I see my classroom students' eyeballs light up when they understand a new concept. What a true blessing to see your own child's lightbulbs go on!

A major ego buster was exactly that—putting my ego aside and learning to parent differently. I didn't even know I had an ego until I had to let go of it. The *blessing* was that I learned I didn't know it all. I wasn't the end all, be all. I learned how to be more humble and how to be a student and not only a teacher. What a gift to be more humble and less controlling. What a lifelong blessing.

An emotional valley I didn't anticipate living through was the loss of my marriage and the breakdown of my family. The *blessing* in that lesson was learning I should have been leaning on my Rock, my Lord, and not expecting my husband to be that rock. I also learned that I had a lot to learn about relationships. They are fluid and evolving, and I must learn to evolve as they do. I now know where I should go when the world can't be there for me. And the world will continue to let me down. What a blessing it is to know where I should go when that happens!

Finally, the challenge of balancing being a mom to two completely differently wired children is always on the forefront of my mind. I have learned that although they are individuals, they are both perfectly created. I have also come to realize both of my children need alone time with me. I once read that love to every child, autistic or not, is spelled T-I-M-E, not L-O-V-E.

I have a tremendous amount of gratitude that I was able to take time off of work and find the resources and therapists to help my son. When I did decide to go back to work, I was fortunate that it was financially feasible to only work part-time so I could carve out even more minutes to help my son with his therapies. We chose to sacrifice my hefty salary in those early days of autism. We had to eat at home a lot more and go out a lot less. But we figured it out. Looking back, we may have sacrificed things, but we really didn't need those things to begin with. And the Lord has provided. "And my God will meet all your needs according to the riches of His glory in Christ Jesus" (Philippians 4:19).

Everybody has a different set of circumstances, and I do not pretend to understand what yours are. I do know, however, the more parents can sacrifice in the early years of their child's development, the better future they can procure for their kid. Time is of the essence when autism is diagnosed. When I wasn't physically with Anthony, I made sure that whoever was with him worked on his behaviors. I taught them how to do that. I made sure Anthony was *in therapy* with his grandparents, cousins, and babysitters. Most families must work because of financial responsibilities. Many working, lower- and middle-class families are already sacrificing. Whether you come from a double-income family with no choice but for both parents to work or a single-parenting family barely making ends meet, every parent can still make a difference in their child's life. Every parent, working or stay-at-home, can find resources and learn skills to help their son or daughter. Every parent can also teach others those skills so that when they are not around, the caregiver can provide therapy to their child. No matter what cards you have been dealt or what circumstance you may be facing, the key is to *never give up!* Don't give up on your child, your hope for a brighter future, or your faith. I know it is a struggle, but it is doable. And ultimately, it is necessary. In the final chapters of my book, I provide you with many resources to help you in that journey of never giving up. This is not an exhaustive list, but it is a great place to begin.

Just recalling those early challenges has been overwhelming. But I didn't overcome any of them alone. I don't know how anybody could. I found my strength, courage, words, and hope because I found Him. I have a peace because I have a promise. I have many promises from a steadfast, loving God, whom I thank many times each day. The best part is that I'm not the only one who has Him. I have taught my children that they have Him as well. It is evident when my autistic boy is struggling with his emotions and behaviors and regulating his temper and then looks up and says, "Help me, God." He's not only my God. He is our God, and He has helped not only me but also my son and daughter. That's His promise. I'm proud to say. I undoubtedly believe Him.

Those early days playing in my perfect world with my perfect dolls are very vibrant memories. I loved creating new outfits, new stories, and new memories with my paper dolls and my Barbie dolls. I guess it's not that much different with my own family. I am creating new stories and new memories every day with them. They inspire me to be a better mom, guiding them to be the best little people they can be. I'm not always perfect in my parenting, and that's okay too. I am doing the very best I can with my perfectly imperfect world.

I am learning. I yearn for a deeper understanding of helping my son and my daughter on their secular journeys as well as their spiritual ones. I am searching for a deeper understanding on my earthly ventures. I want to help others learn about this disorder and spread some hope along the way.

Sometimes I cry, but those tears are not filled with anxiety about my child's future. They are tears of gratitude for the character traits I've developed because of my children. They are tears of love, not worry. It's hard to worry about a perfect plan.

Sometimes I lie in bed, exhausted. Then I think of how far we have come, not only in progress and skills but in character and in spirit. Sometimes I feel overwhelmed, but then I look up and find my strength in Him and realize I am never alone in anything I do.

A lot of the time, I smile, I laugh, I live, and I love. I worry less. I trust more. I learned to learn. I learned to listen more and talk less.

I applaud you for wanting to learn more as well, more about autism, families, character, and faith. I trust you will find your way just as I have. After all, it's a perfect plan for you too. Have a blessed journey!

Dear heavenly Father,

Thank You for so many things. You know my heart inside and out. You know the anxiety and worry I carried around and sometimes pick up from time to time now. I want to thank You for allowing me to see You in the midst of my circumstances and to feel Your strength and Your gentleness in my challenges.

I want to thank You for all of those challenges. It is exactly those trials that led me to You. I have learned to enjoy my life more and worry less, and the unknown is not weighing me down quite like it used to. Thank You for showing me how to enjoy the "what is."

You have always put the perfect people in our lives to help us navigate the world of autism. Always.

Thank You.

Because of Your Word, I know I'm not in control. You are. I am relieved for that.

Thank You again.

What started out as unanswered questions and an unknown future is really part of a perfectly designed plan. I want to thank You for allowing me to take a glimpse of how You have weaved some of those pieces together for us.

Thank You, Lord, for helping me to teach my children more about You. When I hear my daughter asking if she can go to winter church camp and if she can bring her friends to church services, my heart smiles. When I hear my son ask You for help in the midst of his frustrations, my heart melts. When my husband thanks me for praying for him, my soul soars. You are enough. You always have been.

Thank You, Jesus.
Amen.

Part 2

RESOURCES

This section includes information on the following topics:

- General Education v. Special Education
- Individual Education Plans (IEPs)
- What Happens When I Don't Fit In?
- Where to Turn for More Information

Chapter 1

GENERAL EDUCATION V.
SPECIAL EDUCATION

To be completely honest with you, the first chapters of the book discussing the emotional aspect of parenting were challenging to write. I shared my heart in hopes of helping you face similar challenges. My prayer is that you found the hope and inspiration you needed somewhere in my story.

The remainder of the book is more of a resource guide to help with the school issues you may be forced to face when dealing with a special needs child. This was far more tedious and daunting to address because it has to do with school questions, individualized educational plans, parental rights, and places to go when seeking services for your child. It shifts from sharing my heart to sharing my head. The wisdom and facts I gained from living and walking this path hopefully will help you make the crucial choices involving your child's education. I hope you find this section useful and helpful as you travel down the critical road of education.

Every parent who is blessed to have a special needs child will have to make the decision to mainstream their sons or daughters within the general education population or to keep them within the special education population in SDC (special day classes). This

111

decision may very well be one of the most important decisions parents will have to make. In essence, it will determine the path of growth academically, socially, and emotionally for their children for the rest of their lives. The decision, therefore, should not be taken lightly. Nor should it be left solely in the hands of the school personnel. Parents have more of a voice in this decision-making process than they may think they have. They should have a say because, of course, they are the people who know their children the best. They are the people who live with their children day in and day out through the happy, joyful moments as well as the challenging, difficult times. They are the children's best advocates. Selecting an appropriate placement involves considering your overall goals and expectations along with your child's current skill set.

When faced with the difficult decision to include Anthony within the mainstream population or to keep him in the special day classes, many thoughts ran through my mind simultaneously. Keep in mind that my occupation is in education, so I am able to see this situation through the eyes of a teacher and a former assistant principal. However, from a parent's point of view, it is much different. This is my child, and the decisions I make today will affect his tomorrow. Although I have always deeply cared for my students and done what I believed was best for them, my parent's heart took over when it came to my son.

What if I make the wrong choice?
What if I pick the incorrect path for his life?
What if he doesn't seem to be progressing?
What then? What do I do?

Numerous variables came into play to help determine my son's placement. I wanted him to be on par socially and academically with his peers. My long-term goal for him was complete independence for all levels of life. I wanted him to follow directions like everybody else was expected to. I wanted him to be a typical kid or at least as typical as he could be, given his special circumstances. Doesn't every parent want those things? I was no different. Those were my goals for him. Was he capable of meeting them? I believed he was. I tried to teach him that he was.

I started by never giving my son any excuses. I pushed him hard and expected him to rise to the same level of expectations I had set for my daughter. I gave him more support along the way. I never lowered my standards or expectations of him.

In addition, I tried teaching him that he could do anything if he set his mind to it. I remember there were many phrases I used with him in the midst of teaching him confidence. We always said, "I can," not, "I can't." We always used language like "I'll try," "Please help me," and "Help me, God" instead of, "It's too hard" and "I can't do it." There came a time where I had to teach him to say things such as, "it's too difficult," or "I don't like that." It was a fine balance between teaching him respect for others and self-advocating skills. But that's the same with any child, disability or not.

As a teacher in my own classroom, I have always had high expectations of each and every student I've had the blessing of teaching. I have had the privilege and opportunity of teaching EL (English learners), RSP (resource special education students), at-risk students, as well as GATE (gifted and talented students), sometimes all in the same class at the same time. No excuses. We all had to figure it out. For some it was easier, and for others I know it was definitely more challenging. Nevertheless, we had to figure it out. Sometimes modifications and accommodations may have been necessary to help my lower-achieving students. Other times more challenging and in-depth studies needed to be explored to keep the interest of my eager-beaver higher-achieving pupils. Sometimes my higher-achieving students helped my at-risk students. Nevertheless, we figured it out. I kept the standards and expectations high, and I adjusted the support along the way. We all learned. Maybe differently sometimes, but we figured it out together.

Why shouldn't my home be the same way? It should, with a little more love and discipline sprinkled in. Keep my expectations high and adjust the support as needed with each child. Having looked at my classroom experience and knowledge of working with children, I continued with the pedagogy of thinking every child can learn, even the ones who are different, even the students who need more assistance. Even mine. Even the ones with autism.

I expected the classroom teacher to hold Anthony to the same expectations as I did. I wanted to keep the behavioral standards and objectives high while providing academic support where he needed it. Teacher placement and willingness is key to ensure that this occurs. Not all teachers are willing to keep expectations high for students such as mine because they will have to work much harder and perhaps even adjust how much the other students may have to sacrifice along the way.

Anthony was able to learn from others, a skill hard to find naturally within some autistic children. Many autistic children do not naturally learn from their peers or their environments. They are unaware of what others are doing. Therefore, they cannot easily learn from others. They are not motivated by others. Therefore, they do not seek to follow in their footsteps. For some, they do not get the same social reinforcement from interaction with others that typical children receive. On one hand, that is a gift because negative pressure such as drinking and smoking won't be a problem because of the fact that some autistic children may not feel the need to do what others do to please them or gain acceptance. On the other hand, not being able to learn naturally from others leaves you a blank whiteboard with the only written script being that which is programmed into your brain by therapists and trained personnel.

Anthony *was* able to look around and see what others were doing. He didn't always do the right thing because others were, but he had the skill of learning from others. He needed to be motivated to choose to do the right thing.

Because Anthony was able to learn from his peers, I had to decide if I wanted him to learn from typical developing children or not. Of course I did. I wanted him involved in a classroom where typical developing children were sitting, raising their hands, attending to their teacher, and being responsible. If he had lacked the skill of learning from others, I may not have opted for general education. I may have instead chosen a smaller class with more individualized instruction. In addition to those variables, special day classes vary from school to school and from district to district. Some classes and teachers keep expectations high and try to grow the student at each possible interval. Some do not. I did not find one that entailed both of those characteristics. I was searching for a school maintaining high expectations as well as stretching and growing my son's ability to function socially. These were both vital components I needed to see and feel comfortable with before choosing a small classroom. It is a hard combination to acquire because it is very challenging to teach a group of students with different learning disabilities as well as learning styles in the same class. Each student is on his or her own individualized educational plan (IEP). (These plans will be discussed in a future chapter.) It is extremely challenging for a teacher to meet the needs and requirements laid out for every child.

When I visited and investigated the special programs and SDC classes, I found they did not have the characteristics I needed for Anthony. This discovery along with the fact that he can learn from his peers led me to choose the general education path. In the general education class, I was assured that typical developing peers would surround him. I was assured that on a daily basis he would be immersed in the regular classroom, watching and observing typical behaviors and typical instruction. (In kindergarten, it was three and a half hours a day, and in primary school, it was up to seven hours a day.)

When selecting an appropriate path for your child, consider the following:

1. What is my long-term goal for my child?
2. What program will best accomplish that goal?
3. Do I want him or her in smaller classes with others who may have learning disabilities? They may get more individualized instruction, but will they be held to the same behavioral and academic standards?
4. What is my child's current skill set? Would he or she be able to learn and grow within the general education population, or is the child academically too far behind and would need remediation in order to bridge the gap?
5. Can he or she learn from peers?
6. What programs does my district offer for my child?
7. Ask to visit the classes when students are present.
8. Talk with the teachers and request certain teachers you feel may be best for your child if possible.
9. Ask if you can switch into a more effective program at any time during the year.
10. Find out the behavioral expectations in SDC classes and within the general education classes.

Beyond asking questions, I also went into the classes and observed the teaching. I watched how the adults interacted with the students, and I began to get a feel for where Anthony would best fit and where he would best learn.

I took a breath, many breaths. I said a prayer, many prayers, and sent him to kindergarten. I sent him to a regular education kindergarten class with typical developing peers and a teacher with the same expectations for my child as she had for her other students. He did not attend this kindergarten class alone, however. He was accompanied by an aide who helped him with his behaviors and his attention. He went to a general education kindergarten class with prayers, hope, and an aide.

The aide who accompanied my child was his behavioral therapist, the man we had secured for in-home therapy services.

The school and the behavioral therapist blended a program together that included home, school, and community to help generalize my son's skills across all environments. My son had a hard time transferring the new skills being taught at home into the school setting. The hope was if the same therapy team accompanied him into the classroom and taught his teacher the best ways to deal with his behaviors, then he would generalize his skills in both settings. He learned to do just that.

Many districts have their own instructional aides to help in this area. There are two main types of instructional aides— one-on-one aides and collaborative aides. A one-on-one aide is there for solely one child. This aide helps him work through any behaviors and provide academic support. This person might follow the child around throughout the school day, making sure the student is making the correct behavior choices on campus as well as helping to redirect him or her in class. The upside to this aide is that he or she acts as a safety net, if you will, to ensure behaviors remain in check and that redirection and reteaching takes place if needed. The downside to this choice is that the child learns to rely on the aide and not the teacher. The child learns to follow orders from two individuals in the classroom, and that in itself may be overwhelming. I have also noticed that it hinders the child's own processing and thinking for him or herself because the kid doesn't have to do that. He or she only needs to follow what the aide tells him or her to do. So you can see one-on-one aides can have many benefits as well as limitations.

Collaborative aides may be in the classroom, but they are not solely there for one student. They may help other students and even the teacher on other projects. They give the students more independence and offer a safety net in the event the teacher cannot deal with a behavior or a redirection at the moment. They may take the students out to reteach or even to read a test to them if they have auditory issues. They can help support both the student and the teacher without being as invasive as a one-on-one aide.

Kindergarten came and went. So did first, second, and third grades. He attended only general education classes and had general education teachers with high expectations. Around fourth grade we began to accommodate his work to make it more manageable and meaningful. That will be discussed further in future chapters. He was successful in kindergarten and learned to adapt in his class. His teacher learned new techniques to keep him motivated and engaged. I learned how to advocate for my son to be in a general education class. The other students learned not every kid is like them.

These are such important lessons for everybody. Again, I will say I have seen that God works for the good to those who believe. Through this single decision of placing my son in a general education class, everybody learned many gifts of life. My son, his teachers, countless students, and I, all learned new perspectives of life. We learned how to be patient, creative, helpful, caring, and loving. God is good. God is faithful. God works through each and every one of us for one another and for Him.

Each child is different, and every child's needs are varied. There is much to think about when choosing the educational road for your child. Visit many classrooms and talk with many teachers. Trust you will choose the right path for your child. You can always change placements if the one you choose isn't challenging enough or perhaps a bit too much for your child. Enjoy the process and watch the gifts unfold.

> *And we know that God causes all things to work together for good to those who love God, to those who are called according to His purpose.*
>
> *—Romans 8:28*

> *Because of the Lord's great love we are not consumed, for his compassions never fail. They are new every*

morning; great is your faithfulness. I say to myself, "The Lord is my portion; therefore I will wait for him." The Lord is good to those whose hope is in him, it is good to wait quietly for the salvation of the Lord.

—*Lamentations 3:22–26*

Chapter 2

INDIVIDUAL EDUCATION PLANS (IEPS)

Placing Anthony in a general education classroom was difficult not only for him and the school but also for me. The assessments, goals, and services that followed that decision will be discussed in this chapter, but first, I want to describe the scene as I viewed it prior to the paperwork process. I share some of my insights because despite the hardships of "not fitting in," the wisdom of advocating for my son far outweighed the challenges.

More than seven hundred students at my children's elementary school attend class every day. Parents sit patiently in their cars to drop off their kids and start their busy days. Other busy parents walk their children from parked spaces across the crosswalks and onto school grounds. Some carry their kids' backpacks. Some walk with other adults while their children chat on the way to the school grounds. Moms laugh and talk peacefully, knowing that their children won't dart across into the street into merging morning traffic. They have this inner peace because they know they have taught their kids to look both ways, watch for oncoming traffic, and wait until it's safe before crossing. This peace has somehow subconsciously settled into these mom's souls. You can see it on their faces and in their stance.

I didn't quite look like that dropping off my child at school. I didn't have the time to chat with friends because I was always busy chasing my son around. I didn't look calm or even act calm. I looked as if I had an attention disorder myself because my mouth would be chatting with the teacher or another mother, but my eyes and my attention would be focused on Anthony. Frequently, I felt like I was all over the board, and it was probably because I was.

Although some parents may wonder if their children are getting a good education or if the homework load is appropriate, classroom placement, services available, trained personnel, goals, objectives, assessments, and testing are not variables on their minds on a daily basis. When I sent my typical developing daughter to school, my thoughts were very different than when I sent Anthony to school. Suddenly, my mind revolved around the services available, the best placement for him, and what else I could be doing to help him. My feelings usually were those of doubt and anxiety.

When I sent my daughter to school, my thoughts seemed to ebb and flow around various issues.

I hope she likes school.

I want her to grow and learn and be the best Ally she can be.

I hope her teacher is one who motivates but also has high expectations for her.

I hope she enjoys lunchtime and recess.

I hope she makes friends.

I hope she does well.

I hope she is happy.

My feelings that followed those thoughts were usually joyful, content, and peaceful. When I sent my son to school, my thoughts never seemed to rest. In fact, I probably can't write a book long enough to express my concerns.

I hope I choose the right placement (general education over special day class).

I hope he doesn't elope (run away from situation).

I hope he sits down long enough to attend to the lesson.

I hope he pays attention.

I hope he stays safe throughout the day.

I hope his teacher has patience for him.

As I am dropping him off, I hope he doesn't dart into the street.

I hope he can learn from others.

I hope kids are nice to him.

I hope he can be accepted.

I hope he can learn something.

I hope he can speak his thoughts.

I hope he doesn't hit anyone or kick or spit or throw or lick his hands or ...

I hope his behavior aide who shadows him at school isn't sick.

I hope I don't get a call from the school.

I hope I don't have to take another day off of work.

I hope they work on his goals.

I hope!

I hope!

I hope!

There was a lot of hoping going on when I would send him to school. In fact, I didn't look as relaxed as those other parents with café lattes in their hands, laughing and chatting with one another. I probably looked quite anxious with a lot of questions and concerns floating around in my head. That's because it was precisely how I felt—anxious, concerned, scared, and doubtful.

Those early days of making decisions about school placement were very difficult and challenging for me. He didn't look like or act like any other kid in a general education classroom. I didn't look or act like any typical mother in a sea of normal typical parents, but nevertheless, I plunged forward with my prayers and chose to place Anthony in general education, also known as inclusion, over a special education class. Intellectually knowing he probably wouldn't quite fit in with the masses. Nor would I.

I stepped out in faith, and with hope, I then placed him in the best place I felt was right for him.

Regardless of where your child is placed, you'll have to deal with IEPs. I dread writing or even thinking about Anthony's IEPs. IEPs are "individual education plans" written by a team of individuals to best meet the needs of a child with special needs.

The IEP meeting is designed so that assessment, testing, and current levels of achievement are being addressed and discussed. From those assessments and current levels of performance, goals are formulated so that the student can work specifically on weak areas and the school personnel support staff and parents can focus on those areas when teaching that child.

The team is usually comprised of a school administrator, a special education teacher, a general education teacher, and any other support staff needed, such as occupational therapists or speech therapists and parents. The IEP meeting can be a great tool in helping a student bridge the gap they may have in learning, or it can be the fight of your life in securing services for your child. In my case, it has always been the latter.

Parents may often feel they do not know what is best for their children and defer to what the school IEP team states may be best. The first thing I would share is that I would encourage parents to *research, read, investigate, and speak* to professionals so they can walk into IEP meetings with knowledge and confidence. The need to legally apprise myself on the correct terminology to request services (services I didn't even know existed) was overwhelming at times. Even to write about it is overwhelming. To advocate for it *yearly* is intimidating and exhausting but necessary.

What I believe most parents may not understand is that they have a *voice* at their children's IEP meetings. Although teachers, school administration, and other support staff may be experts in their fields, parents are the experts in their sons or daughters' lives. They live with them day in and day out. They know at their core if there are concerns in certain areas. With both eyes open and being careful to keep denial and irrational wishes for the children out of the picture, they also have a good grasp of their children's needs.

In addition to having a *voice* in the meetings, many parents do not know they may bring in their own private specialist's summaries, recommendations, and assessments. As a parent, I paid for clinical speech therapists, occupational therapists, behavior therapists, and neurologist's assessments of my son's diagnosis, prognosis, and recommendations. In some states, parents may request that their school district pay for a private professional assessment (speech, OT, behavioral) so they do not have to pay the cost out of their own pocket. I asked the IEP team to take my private assessments into consideration when determining goals and services for my son. My doctors of choice were truthful and honest in their assessments. They were able to help in a clinical setting and not only an educational one. They were able to assess him and treat him in ways many educators were not professionally or clinically trained to do. Parents are not simply at the mercy of what their school site states and their school employees assess.

In many cases, privately paid professionals may agree with the recommendations the school offers. Then the parents can rest assured their children are receiving what many professionals feel is adequate and best. In other cases, there may be different, more intense services available for a parent's child—services perhaps the parents or even the schools didn't know existed. In those cases, they can shine a light on the IEP and have the team consider those services and recommendations as well. Perhaps the school has the capability of providing some of these services or finding a way to provide something similar. In either case, *parents have a voice, and they can always get a second opinion from a clinical professional for their children.* They are active members of the IEP team and should be treated as such.

Other details that parents may not be aware are in their realm of influence include the following:

- They may audiotape the IEP meetings with advance written notification to school personnel. This may be helpful in case they want to replay the notes of the meeting for clarification purposes or need to go to a due process hearing if items of importance are being disputed.
- They may bring in their own personal assessments to be considered by the IEP team as stated earlier.
- They can and should request a copy of their procedural rights and safeguards.
- They can request that goals be written into the IEP even if the teachers did not write them out initially.
- There is a specific procedure to be followed and adhered to in IEP meetings. Parents should be aware of their state's procedures and make sure they are being followed. Otherwise districts can be out of compliance with the process.
- Parents may add their own opinions and concerns to the IEP notes. The notes are not only those of the educational participants.
- Parents may search out their rights and any services provided by their local Regional Centers and request that such services be provided.
- Parents may request an IEP to be held more than one time a year.
- Parents may request to see district assessments and proposed goals prior to IEP meetings to review.
- Parents may request teachers give/provide the current progress of their children at any time.
- Parents should be aware that there is a legal timeline that assessments must follow. Parents should also consider putting every request in writing. Those written request put the legal timeline in motion. It is also proof that such requests were actually made. Requests for your child's

assessments, progress reports, or services should *always* be put in writing.

There are many resources, advocates, and parent information websites available on the Internet. Local regional centers are places to visit as well. Private, clinical support staff, such as: speech pathologists, occupational and behavioral therapists, nutrition and wellness centers, developmental pediatricians, and neurologists, are avenues parents can and should exhaust.

I leave this chapter with a couple of words of caution.

- Request everything in writing from any entity from which you desire a service.
- Read, reread, and then read it again before signing anything for your approval. I often take home my son's IEPs for a couple of weeks and place a few different sets of eyes on it prior to returning it with a signature. Once it is signed, it has been legally agreed to. I reread it and make any necessary corrections with the district prior to signing it for approval.

Individual education plans are part of every special needs child's life. They are designed to help children succeed. However, they can be intimidating and challenging simultaneously. *Prepare, read, research, and seek* those whom you trust with helping you build a plan you are happy with for your child. Parents have rights. They need to research them.

My son's IEPs are lengthy. They require time-consuming meetings where every person is being held accountable for making my child's education the best they can. I bring in private assessments and request district reports with goals and assessments (in writing) ahead of time so I can review them. I ask a lot of questions and document everything. I audiotape my IEP meetings for accountability and factual integrity. I have the final copy of the IEP read and reread for accuracy. I often do not finish the IEP in one meeting. My son has a relentless mom who makes sure no stone goes unturned in finding the keys to his success.

It's hard!

It's intimidating!

It's challenging!

It's like walking through a parking lot on any given school day morning and not fitting in and watching my kid not fit in.

It's hard!

It's intimidating!

It's challenging!

But my son receives the services he deserves, and I have many professionals agreeing with me. I can put my head on the pillow and rest assured that my prayers are being answered—no matter how hard, how intimidating, how challenging it may be.

I often reflect back to those early days and wonder where the drive and strength came from. What made it possible to fight those fights, research those questions, and hold my head up high when so many others cocked theirs to the side?

I can do all this through Him who gives me strength.

—Philippians 4:13

For we are God's handiwork, created in Christ Jesus to do good works, which God prepared in advance for us to do.

—Ephesians 2:10

But thanks be to God, who always leads us as captives in Christ's triumphal procession and uses us to spread the aroma of knowledge of him everywhere.

—2 Corinthians 2:14

In all these things we are more than conquerors through him who loved us.

—Romans 8:37

Chapter 3

WHAT HAPPENS WHEN
I DON'T FIT IN?

After deciding to place my son in a general education classroom with typical developing students, I soon realized we would eventually have to deal with the issues of not fitting in. I knew Anthony was different. I also knew other kids might not *get* him. I knew we would have to deal with

- teasing,
- taunting,
- bullying,
- exclusion, and
- snickering

We would have to confront these and a host of other issues. I knew these things would occur because I am a teacher. I single-handedly observe kids being cruel to others who are not like them. Perhaps they don't have the right hair color, the popular clothes, or even the right speech. Nevertheless, the more different from the norm one is, the more intolerant others may be of them. I knew Anthony was different, and I knew we would have to deal with it sooner or later.

This path is not an easy road to walk as a parent. We don't want to face the fact that our child may not be accepted because of a disorder or disability he or she had no hand in choosing. We thirst for our child not only to be accepted but celebrated and adored. If you go to the football games and other sporting events, parents are yelling and cheering because they are proud of their star athletes. Equally so, if you attend awards ceremonies, parents are doting over their students of the month chosen for academic excellence by their teachers. Every parent I have met wants to know their kids are thriving and accepted by their peers. It's a natural reaction. My hope is that I can share different coping strategies. I was worried my son would not be protected from others excluding him, laughing at his odd behaviors, and ridiculing him in front of others. However, I remember asking myself these questions: *Who of us is guaranteed protection from those things? Are we ever protected from people making fun of us and making us feel badly about who we are?*

Then I answered myself, as I often do, "We aren't protected in life from those things. There are no guarantees that we will have an easy road and complete acceptance from others." In fact, many of us had to deal with

- not fitting in,
- not being good enough,
- not wearing the right clothes,
- not looking the right way,
- not having our parents drive the nicest cars,
- not being the best on the team,
- not winning the spelling bee,
- not having the right haircut,
- not utilizing the best and the brightest technology,
- not getting the highest grades,
- not having the right skin color, and
- not speaking the right language.

And the list goes on. As adults, it doesn't get any easier. We might have experienced

- not attending the most prestigious college,
- not driving the most luxurious car,
- not residing in the most attractive neighborhood,
- not owning the purebred puppy,
- not bringing home the biggest paycheck, and
- not living in the most extravagant home.

And that list goes on.

If we assess our value on what others think of us, we will always fall short. Our culture and society places a very high standard on what we own, our economic status, and our positions of influence. That's why many of us are consumed with how we look, what possessions we own, and where we fit in in the big scope of life. I have learned not to measure my worth based on how others view me. Instead I measure my worth on how the Lord views me. From this perspective, I want to please Him, and I'm not so concerned about pleasing the world.

From this perspective, I also had to teach Anthony how to recognize if someone wasn't being nice to him and then how to handle the situation if and when it arose. His challenge came during second grade. It was the point where kids begin to notice differences among themselves. They begin to notice who is like them and who is different. They notice the difference in clothing, language, and physical appearance. It's also the point where if you don't blend in, then you stand out. The light was shed on his differences, and he began being teased because of them.

I didn't hear it from him, largely because of the fact that he wasn't aware it was happening. He had no idea that boys in his class were making jokes at his expense. He really didn't understand what jokes even were. When others would laugh at him, he would laugh with them, which in turn would increase the teasing and the taunting. I heard the news from his behavioral aides who would accompany him to school. Of course, they would tell the other students to be nice to him; however, it was only a Band-Aid for such a larger gusher.

Some kids didn't accept him. Some continued to make fun of him. Some laughed at him and excluded him from their groups and their activities. The single most disturbing part for me was that he was completely unaware of it. He didn't recognize that his peers were using him for the target of their jokes.

Although I was heartbroken, I had been expecting this, so I had a plan. I handled the situation twofold. First, I had to teach Anthony what *mean* looked like and felt like. Secondly, I had to teach the other kids what *autism* looked like. Teaching Anthony what *mean* looked like and how it felt to be teased was no easy task. We had to use visuals and pictures of people being mean to one another to show him what *mean* looked like. We taught him what being excluded looked like by excluding him from what we were doing. It was hard. It was sad. We role-played activities where I got his cousins and other family members to call him names, and then we taught him how to stand up for himself. At first, we explained to him we were going to be teaching him these things so that we wouldn't damage the confidence and self-esteem we had worked so desperately to build up. After a while, we had to see if he was able to stand up for himself without prompting him. That was the hard part. It was difficult finding parents who would allow me to use their kids to help with the role-playing activities. However, once I explained to them that this approach was the way Anthony learned best and that they were helping him, they were far more willing to accommodate us.

It was an arduous task. You see, my concern was more about teaching him to protect and advocate for himself than trying to have him fit in. Anthony eventually learned what name-calling, exclusion, and bullying looked like. He was able to convey this to the teachers and principal when he felt like he was encountering those challenges. It didn't happen overnight, and it was a lengthy process. But he learned how to stand up for himself. Today he will occasionally put his mother in check if I'm raising my voice, letting me know, "It's not very nice to speak to me in that tone." Wow, that boomerang comes back around doesn't it!

Next, I had to educate the students. I asked the principal if I could speak to the students in Anthony's class so that they would understand some of the reasons he behaved the way he did. The principal said, "Absolutely!" He trusted my insight as a teacher and knew the kids would have a greater understanding if they heard from an autistic child's mother.

I explained to them what it meant to be autistic in words that seven-year-olds could understand. They asked a lot of questions, and I did my best to answer them. They began to understand Anthony a bit better.

It helped them to see certain facts.
Different ... doesn't equal weird.
Different ... doesn't equal dumb.
Different ... doesn't equal scary.
Different just means different.

They also began to grasp that Anthony, although different in some ways from them, wasn't different in *all* ways. He, too, wanted acceptance, friendship, and love. They began to accept his differences, and some even began to help him. They grew to understand that he needed a little extra help in some things and a bit more patience with other things. It was wonderful seeing kids who had once been so unsure of him grow to help and accept him.

After educating the students in my son's class, it was easy to see the need for more school-wide curriculum to teach everyone acceptance skills. I've spoken with several families about the importance of teaching their special child how to self-advocate for themselves. I enjoy consulting with families and sharing what

I've learned with them. It makes me feel like I am giving back to others what I have been given.

I'm also continuing to teach my son to advocate for himself and get his needs met. Sometimes I'm the teacher to Anthony, and other times I am his student. He has helped me to help him *and* to help others. He has helped me to reach out to others and teach them about mental disorders and about overcoming those disabilities. He has also helped me to teach people how to become better friends with one another and never allow people to walk the school halls alone. Kids have told me they feel great about themselves when they stand up for others. What a gift that has been for me, for them, and for kids like my boy! What is this thing about *not fitting in* anyways?

> *So in everything, do to others what you would have them do to you, for this sums up the Law and the Prophets.*
>
> *—Matthew 7:12*

Chapter 4

WHERE TO TURN FOR
MORE INFORMATION

There is a wealth of information available for parents, teachers, and professionals on the subject of developmental disabilities and autism. Some of the techniques I have learned to manage my son's behaviors have come directly from professionals teaching me and through hands-on experience. However, learning how to manage autism and the laws simultaneously have come directly from researching websites and reading many books on the topic. Some of the most invaluable resources provided a base for what I have included in this final chapter. This list is by no means exhaustive. These are only a few resources available to you, but remember there is a sea of information for those willing to explore it!

The State of California Department of Developmental Services

This website includes laws, regulations, facts, and statistics on developmental disabilities within the state of California. The California Department of Developmental Services is also the agency through which the state of California provides services and supports to individuals with developmental disabilities. These services are provided by state-operated developmental centers and community centers that contract with twenty-one local regional centers. One can find a local regional center in their area on the site as well. Finally, the website offers answers to questions such as the following: Who is eligible for services? What programs are available for my child? How do I get an accurate diagnosis? Visit www.dds.ca.gov.

Important Laws

Lanterman Developmental Disability Services Act

"The Lanterman Developmental Disabilities Services Act, known as the 'Lanterman Act,' is an important piece of legislation that was passed in 1969. This is the California law that says people with developmental disabilities and their families have a right to get the services and supports they need to live like people without disabilities. The Lanterman Act outlines the rights of individuals with developmental disabilities and their families, how the regional centers and service providers can help these individuals, what services and supports they can obtain, how to use the individualized program plan to get needed services, what to do when someone violates the Lanterman Act, and how to improve the system" (http://www.lanterman.org).

Section 4512 of the California Welfare and Institutions Code

The following is an excerpt from Chapter 1.6: General Provisions:

> "Developmental disability" means a disability that originates before an individual attains eighteen years of age; continues, or can be expected to continue, indefinitely; and constitutes a substantial disability for that individual. As defined by

the Director of Developmental Services, in consultation with the Superintendent of Public Instruction, this term shall include intellectual disability, cerebral palsy, epilepsy, and autism. This term shall also include disabling conditions found to be closely related to intellectual disability or to require treatment similar to that required for individuals with an intellectual disability, but shall not include other handicapping conditions that are solely physical in nature.

(b) "Services and supports for persons with developmental disabilities" means specialized services and supports or special adaptations of generic services and supports directed toward the alleviation of a developmental disability or toward the social,

personal, physical, or economic habilitation or rehabilitation of an individual with a developmental disability, or toward the achievement and maintenance of independent, productive, and normal lives. The determination of which services and supports are necessary for each consumer shall be made through the individual program plan process.

The determination shall be made on the basis of the needs and preferences of the consumer or, when appropriate, the consumer's family, and shall include consideration of a range of service options proposed by individual program plan participants, the effectiveness of each option in meeting the goals stated in the individual program plan, and the cost-effectiveness of each option.

Services and supports listed in the individual program plan may include, but are not limited to, diagnosis, evaluation, treatment, personal care, daycare, domiciliary care, special living arrangements, physical, occupational, and speech therapy, training, education, supported and sheltered employment, mental health services, recreation, counseling of the individual with a developmental disability and of his or her family, protective and other social and socio-legal services, information and referral services, follow-along services, adaptive equipment and supplies, advocacy assistance, including self-advocacy training, facilitation and peer advocates, assessment, assistance in locating a home, child care, behavior training and behavior modification programs, camping, community integration services, community support, daily living skills training, emergency and crisis intervention, facilitating circles of support, habilitation, homemaker services, infant stimulation programs, paid roommates, paid neighbors, respite, short-term out-of-home care, social skills training, specialized medical and dental care, supported living arrangements, technical and financial assistance, travel training, training for parents of children with developmental disabilities, training for parents with developmental disabilities, vouchers, and transportation services necessary to ensure delivery of services to persons with developmental disabilities. Nothing in this subdivision is intended to expand or authorize a new or different service or support for any consumer unless that service or support is contained in his or her individual program plan.

(c) Notwithstanding subdivisions (a) and (b), for any organization or agency receiving federal financial participation under the federal Developmental Disabilities Assistance and Bill of Rights Act of 2000, as amended, "developmental disability" and "services for persons with developmental disabilities" mean the terms as defined in the federal act to the extent required by federal law.

(d) "Consumer" means a person who has a disability that meets the definition of developmental disability set forth in subdivision (a).

(e) "Natural supports" means personal associations and relationships typically developed in the community that enhance the quality and security of life for people, including, but not limited to, family relationships, friendships reflecting the diversity of the neighborhood and the community, associations with fellow students or employees in regular classrooms and workplaces, and associations developed through participation in clubs, organizations, and other civic activities.

(f) "Circle of support" means a committed group of community members, who may include family members, meeting regularly with an individual with developmental disabilities in order to share experiences, promote autonomy and community involvement, and assist the individual in establishing and maintaining natural supports. A circle of support generally includes a plurality of members who neither provide nor receive services or supports for persons with developmental disabilities and who do not receive payment for participation in the circle of support.

(g) "Facilitation" means the use of modified or adapted materials, special instructions, equipment, or personal assistance by an individual, such as assistance with communications, that will enable a consumer to understand and participate to the maximum extent possible in the decisions and choices that affect his or her life.

(h) "Family support services" means services and supports that are provided to a child with developmental disabilities or his or her family and that contribute to the ability of the family to reside together.

(i) "Voucher" means any authorized alternative form of service delivery in which the consumer or family member is provided with a payment, coupon, chit, or other form of authorization that enables the consumer or family member to choose his or her own service provider.

(j) "Planning team" means the individual with developmental disabilities, the parents or legally appointed guardian of a minor consumer or the legally appointed conservator of an adult consumer, the authorized representative, including those appointed pursuant to subdivision (d) of Section 4548 and subdivision (e) of Section 4705, one or more regional center representatives, including the designated regional center service coordinator pursuant to subdivision (b) of Section 4640.7, any individual, including a service provider, invited by the consumer, the parents or legally appointed guardian of a minor consumer or the legally appointed conservator of an adult consumer, or the authorized representative, including those appointed pursuant to subdivision (d) of Section 4548 and subdivision (e) of Section 4705, and including a minor's, dependent's, or ward's court-appointed developmental services decision maker appointed pursuant to Section 319, 361, or 726.

(k) "Stakeholder organizations" means statewide organizations representing the interests of consumers, family members, service providers, and statewide advocacy organizations.

(l) "Substantial disability" means the existence of significant functional limitations in three or more of the following areas of major life activity, as determined by a regional center, and as appropriate to the age of the person:

(1) Self-care.

(2) Receptive and expressive language.

(3) Learning.

(4) Mobility.

(5) Self-direction.

(6) Capacity for independent living.

(7) Economic self-sufficiency.

Any reassessment of substantial disability for purposes of continuing eligibility shall utilize the same criteria under which the individual was originally made eligible.

(m) "Native language" means the language normally used or the preferred language identified by the individual and, when appropriate, his or her parent, legal guardian or conservator, or authorized representative.

http://law.onecle.com/california/welfare/4512.html

The Americans with Disabilities Act of 1990

Passed by Congress in 1990, the Americans with Disabilities Act (ADA) is the nation's first comprehensive civil rights law addressing the needs of people with disabilities, prohibiting discrimination in employment, public services, public accommodations, and telecommunications (www.eeoc.gov).

Notice of Procedural Safeguards

The Notice of Procedural Safeguards is information providing parents, legal guardians, and surrogate parents of children with disabilities an overview of their educational rights and safeguards. They can usually be accessed through the website of your individual state's educational government page. Any school district can provide you one as well.

These safeguards, required under the Individuals with Disabilities Education Act (IDEA), must be provided to you

- when you ask for a copy,
- the first time your child is referred for special education assessment,
- each time you are given an assessment plan to evaluate your child,
- upon receipt of the first state or due process complaint in a school year, and
- when the decision is made to make a removal that constitutes a change of placement.

(20 USC 1415[d]; 34 CFR 300.504; EC 56301[d], EC56321, and 56341.1[g] [1])

The Notice of Procedural Safeguards for the state of California are thirteen pages in length and supply a wealth of information to parents and guardians alike.

IDEA

"IDEA is a federal law that requires school districts to provide a "free appropriate public education" (in English, referred to as FAPE) to eligible children with disabilities. A free appropriate public education means that special education and related services are to be provided as described in an individualized education program (in English, known as IEP) and under public supervision to your child at no cost to you" (Notice of Procedural Safeguards CDE).

The Center for Disease Control and Prevention

"From the food you eat, to the air you breathe, to staying safe wherever you are, CDC's mission touches all aspects of daily life. CDC researchers, scientists, doctors, nurses, economists, communicators, educators, technologists, epidemiologists and many other professionals all contribute their expertise to improving public health" (www.cdc.gov).

The National Center on Birth Defects and Developmental Disabilities

"Autism spectrum disorder (ASD) is a group of developmental disabilities that can cause significant social, communication and behavioral challenges. CDC is committed to continuing to provide essential data on ASD, search for factors that put children at risk for ASD and possible causes, and develop resources that help identify children with ASD as early as possible" (http://www. cdc.gov/NCB).

Regional Centers

"Regional centers are nonprofit private corporations that contract with the Department of Developmental Services to provide or coordinate services and supports for individuals with developmental disabilities. They have offices throughout

California to provide a local resource to help find and access the many services available to individuals and their families" (State of California Department of Developmental Services).

Various Therapy Options

Behavioral Therapy

"Behavioral therapy is a treatment that helps change potentially self-destructing behaviors. It is also called behavioral modification or cognitive behavioral therapy. Medical professionals use this type of therapy to replace bad habits with good ones. The therapy also helps you cope with difficult situations" (www.Healthline.com).

Applied Behavior Analysis

The following is an excerpt from the website for the Autism Speaks organization:

> *"Behavior analysis focuses on the principles that explain how learning takes place. Positive reinforcement is one such principle. When a behavior is followed by some sort of reward, the behavior is more likely to be repeated. Through decades of research, the field of behavior analysis has developed many techniques for increasing useful behaviors and reducing those that may cause harm or interfere with learning. Applied behavior analysis (ABA) is the use of these techniques and principles to bring about meaningful and positive change in behavior. As mentioned, behavior analysts began working with young children with autism and related disorders in the 1960s. Early techniques often involved adults directing most of the instruction. Some allowed the child to take the lead. Since that time, a wide variety of ABA techniques have been developed for building useful skills in learners with*

autism – from toddlers through adulthood. These
techniques can be used in structured situations such as
a classroom lesson as well as in "everyday" situations
such as family dinnertime or the neighborhood
playground. Some ABA therapy sessions involve one-
on-one interaction between the behavior analyst and
the participant. Group instruction can likewise prove
useful (www.AutismSpeaks.com).

Occupational Therapy

The following is an excerpt from the website for the American
Occupational Therapy Association:

In its simplest terms, occupational therapists and
occupational therapy assistants help people across
the lifespan participate in the things they want and
need to do through the therapeutic use of everyday
activities (occupations). Common occupational
therapy interventions include helping children with
disabilities to participate fully in school and social
situations, helping people recovering from injury to
regain skills, and providing supports for older adults
experiencing physical and cognitive changes.

Occupational therapy services typically include:

- an individualized evaluation, during which
  the client/family and occupational therapist
  determine the person's goals
- customized intervention to improve the
  person's ability to perform daily activities and
  reach the goals.

- an outcomes evaluation to ensure that the goals are being met and/or make changes to the intervention plan.

Occupational therapy services may include comprehensive evaluations of the client's home and other environments (e.g., workplace, school), recommendations for adaptive equipment and training in its use, and guidance and education for family members and caregivers. Occupational therapy practitioners have a holistic perspective, in which the focus is on adapting the environment to fit the person, and the person is an integral part of the therapy team (http://www.aota.org/MemberCenter.aspx).

Speech and Language Therapy

The following is an excerpt from the website for The American Occupational Therapy Association:

"Speech disorders occur when a person is unable to produce speech sounds correctly or fluently, or has problems with their voice. Language disorders occur when a person has trouble understanding others (receptive language) or sharing thoughts, ideas and feelings completely (expressive language). Speech-language pathologists identify, assess, and treat speech and language problems" (American Speech-Language-Hearing Association, http://www.asha.org/public/).

Nutrition Therapy

The following is a set of claims from the book *The 10-Step Nutrition Plan to Help Treat Your Child's Autism, Asperger's or ADHD*:

> *Improving the nutritional intake of the autistic child can help improve overall health, function and behavior. Nutrition deficiencies, allergies, sensitivities and gastrointestinal disorders are commonly reported in children with autism. The author states little research supports diet to be a cause of symptoms or treatment for autism. Autistic children often have restrictive eating behaviors and problem-feeding behaviors that put them at risk for poor nutrition intake. (Strickland, Elizabeth, MS, RD, LD, Da Capo Lifelong Books, 2009)*

Sensory Integration Therapy

The following is an excerpt from the online version of the official *Journal of the American Academy of Pediatrics*:

> *Sensory-based therapies are increasingly used by occupational therapists and sometimes by other types of therapists in treatment of children with developmental and behavioral disorders. Sensory-based therapies involve activities that are believed to organize the sensory system by providing vestibular, proprioceptive, auditory, and tactile inputs. Brushes, swings, balls, and other specially designed therapeutic or recreational equipment are used to provide these inputs. However, it is unclear whether children who present with sensory-based problems have an actual 'disorder' of the sensory pathways of the brain or whether these deficits are characteristics associated with other developmental and behavioral disorders. Because there is no universally accepted framework for diagnosis, sensory processing disorder generally should not be diagnosed. Other developmental and*

behavioral disorders must always be considered, and a thorough evaluation should be completed. Difficulty tolerating or processing sensory information is a characteristic that may be seen in many developmental behavioral disorders, including autism spectrum disorders, attention-deficit/hyperactivity disorder, developmental coordination disorders, and childhood anxiety disorders (http://pediatrics.aappublications. org/content/early/2012/05/23/peds.2012-0876).

The American Academy of Pediatrics Policy Statement

Sensory Integration Therapies for Children with Developmental and Behavioral Disorders

Please read the very helpful section on complementary and integrative medicine and council on children with disabilities (http://pediatrics.aappublications.org/content/129/6/1186.full).

Play Therapy (Floor Time)

The following is an excerpt from Dr. Stanley Greenspan's website:

The Greenspan Floor time Approach is a system developed by the late Dr. Stanley Greenspan. Floor time meets children where they are and builds upon their strengths and abilities through interacting and creating a warm relationship. It challenges them to go further and to develop who they are rather than what their diagnosis says. In Floor time, you use this time with your child to excite her interests, draw her to connect to you, and challenge her to be creative, curious, and spontaneous—all of which move her forward intellectually and emotionally. (As children get older, Floor time essentially morphs into an exciting, back-and-forth time of exploring the child's ideas.)

For any age child, you do three things:

- *Follow your child's lead, i.e. enter the child's world and join in their emotional flow;*
- *Challenge her to be creative and spontaneous; and*
- *Expand the action and interaction to include all or most of her senses and motor skills as well as different emotions.*

As you do all this, while staying within her focus, you are helping her practice basic thinking skills: engagement, interaction, symbolic thinking and logical thinking. To master these skills requires using all these senses, emotions, and motor skills, as The Greenspan Floortime Approach explains.

Dr. Greenspan developed Floortime to help families support their child's development. Floortime can be done at home or at a clinic, but it's useful, especially at the beginning, to have some guidance from a comprehensive source (www.stanleygreenspan.com/ what-is-floortime/)

Family Counseling Services

This service may be available through insurance carriers as well as for private-paying individuals.

The Bible (any version)

Ask and it will be given to you; seek and you will find; knock and the door will be opened to you. For everyone who asks receives; the one who seeks finds; and to the one who knocks, the door will be opened.

—*Matthew 7:7*

My son, if you accept my words and store up my commands within you, turning your ear to wisdom and applying your heart to understanding~ indeed, if you call out for insight and cry aloud for understanding, and if you look for it as for silver and search for it as for hidden treasure, then you will understand the fear of the Lord and find the knowledge of God. For the Lord gives wisdom; from His mouth come knowledge and understanding.

—Proverbs 2:1–6

Trust in the Lord with all your heart and lean not on your own understanding; in all your ways submit to Him, and He will make your paths straight.

—Proverbs 3:5–6

Now to Him who is able to do immeasurable more than all we ask or imagine, according to His power that is at work within us to Him be glory in the church and in Christ Jesus throughout all generation, for ever and ever! Amen.

—Ephesians 3:20

As for God, his way is perfect: The Lord's word is flawless; he shields all who take refuge in him. For who is God besides the Lord? And who is the Rock except our God? It is God who arms me with strength and keeps my way secure.

—Psalm 18:30–32

Let us not become weary in doing good, for at the proper time we will reap a harvest if we do not give up.

—Galatians 6:9

Look you scoffers, wonder and perish, for I am going to do something in your days that you would never believe, even if someone told you.

—Acts 13:41

Thus the heavens and all the earth were completed in all their vast array. By the seventh day God had finished the work He had been doing; so on the seventh day he rested from all His work. Then God blessed the seventh day and made it holy, because on it He rested from all the work of creating that he had done.

—Genesis 2:1–3

Therefore do not worry about tomorrow, for tomorrow will worry about itself. Each day has enough trouble of its own.

—Matthew 6:34

Then the Lord said to Moses, "Say to the Israelites, 'You must observe my Sabbaths. This will be a sign between me and you for the generations to come, so you may know that I am the Lord, who makes you holy.'"

—Exodus 31:12–13

And my God will meet all your needs according to the riches of His glory in Christ Jesus.

—Philippians 4:19

And we know that in all things God works for the good of those who love Him, who have been called according to His purpose.

—Romans 8:28

People were also bringing babies to Jesus for Him to place His hands on them. When the disciples saw this, they rebuked them. But Jesus called the children to Him and said, "Let the little children come to me, and do not hinder them, for the kingdom of God belongs to such as these.

—Luke 18:15–16

She brings him good, not harm, all the days of her life.

—Proverbs 31:12

Finally, brothers, and sisters, whatever is true, whatever is noble, whatever is right, whatever is pure, whatever is lovely, whatever is admirable~ if anything is excellent or praiseworthy~ think about such things.

—Philippians 4:8

A gentle answer turns away wrath, but a harsh word stirs up anger.

—Proverbs 15:1

He says, "Be still and know that I am God."

—Psalm 46:10

And now these three remain: faith, hope and love. But the greatest of these is love.

—1 Corinthians 13:13

Because of the Lord's great love we are not consumed, for his compassions never fail. They are new every morning; great is your faithfulness. I say to myself, "The Lord is my portion; therefore I will wait for him." The Lord is good to those whose hope is in him, it is good to wait quietly for the salvation of the Lord.

—Lamentations 3:22–26

I can do all this through him who gives me strength.

—Philippians 4: 13

For we are God's handiwork, created in Christ Jesus to do good works, which God prepared in advance for us to do.

—Ephesians 2:10

But thanks be to God, who always leads us as captives in Christ's triumphal procession and uses us to spread the aroma of the knowledge of Him everywhere.

—2 Corinthians 2:14

Iin all these things we are more than conquerors through Him who loved us.

—Romans 8: 37

So in everything, do to others what you would have them do to you, for this sums up the Law and the Prophets.

—Matthew 7:12

Ask and it will be given to you; seek and you will find; knock and the door will be opened to you. For everyone who asks receives; the one who seeks finds; and to the one who knocks, the door will be opened.

—Matthew 7:7

Appendix Scripture Cited in Chapter 11
The Wife of Noble Character

A wife of noble character who can find?

She is worth far more than rubies.

Her husband has full confidence in her and lacks nothing of value.

She brings him good, not harm, all the days of her life.

She selects wool and flax and works with eager hands.

She is like the merchant ships, bringing her food from afar.

She gets up while it is still night; she provides food for her family and portions for her female servants.

She considers a field and buys it; out of her earnings she plants a vineyard.

She sets about her work vigorously; her arms are strong for her tasks.

She sees that her trading is profitable, and her lamp does not go out at night.

In her hand she holds the distaff and grasps the spindle with her fingers.

She opens her arms to the poor and extends her hands to the needy.

When it snows, she has no fear for her household; for all of them are clothed in scarlet.

She makes coverings for her bed; she is clothed in fine linen and purple.

Her husband is respected at the city gate, where he takes his seat among the elders of the land.

She makes linen garments and sells them, and supplies the merchants with sashes.

She is clothed with strength and dignity; she can laugh at the days to come.

She speaks with wisdom, and faithful instruction is on her tongue.

She watches over the affairs of her household and does not eat the bread of idleness.

Her children arise and call her blessed; her husband also, and he praises her:

Many women do noble things, but you surpass them all.

Charm is deceptive, and beauty is fleeting; but a woman who fears the Lord is to be praised.

Honor her for all that her hands have done, and let her works bring her praise at the city gate.

—Proverbs 31:10–31

If you were inspired and encouraged after reading
Inspiration for Autism...A Pathway to Hope and Resources,
I would encourage you to visit www.inspirationforautism.com
for more information.

To inquire about having Debra speak at your
event, webinars, or consulting, also visit
www.inspirationforautism.com and click
on "Speaking and Consulting."